THE GOD STORY

Encountering unfailing love in the
unfolding narrative of Scripture

Adam Cox and Alain Emerson

FORM

First published in Great Britain in 2024

Form
SPCK Group
Studio 101
The Record Hall
16–16A Baldwin's Gardens
London EC1N 7RJ
www.spck.org.uk

British Library Cataloguing-in-Publication Data
A catalogue record for this book is available from the British Library

ISBN 978-0-281-08750-1
eBook ISBN 978-0-281-08749-5

1 3 5 7 9 10 8 6 4 2

Typeset by Fakenham Prepress Solutions, Fakenham, Norfolk NR21 8NL
First printed in Great Britain by Clays Limited

eBook by Fakenham Prepress Solutions, Fakenham, Norfolk NR21 8NL

Contents

We dedicate this book to our children.

Alain: Annie, Erin and Finn; may your hearts burn with love for Jesus and a passion for the Bible all the days of your life.

Adam: My beloved daughters Liliwyn Lesedi, Selah Shore and Noelle Story; I pray you would increasingly know friendship with the Holy Spirit, fascination with Jesus and the unfailing love of the Father.

Foreword

The first time we encountered the *God Story* was not in written words on a page, but in burning hearts, as the message of this book was preached by our longtime friend Adam Cox. We had all the students and staff in our discipleship school crammed into our living room. It was an uncomfortable, people-sitting-everywhere experience that we imagine felt much like the early church would have done: a room full of hunger and expectation. We watched our students hang on each word that was spoken and saw scales falling from their eyes as they saw who God really is. Just like the travellers on the road to Emmaus, our students' hearts were transformed from a state of hopelessness and disappointment to hearts that burned with hope and an expectation.

What a glorious gift it is to believers young and old – the moment when you realize that you are part of a much bigger story: your life is woven into a tapestry that has been in the heart of God since the beginning. That is when you can move from the familiarity of the gospel to fascination with the intention of the heart of God.

We are thrilled that the message we watched change the lives of students year after year is now written by Adam and Alain in the pages of a book that more people can experience. We eagerly expect the moments that are coming for all who read it … knowing that they are loved, chosen, and belong in the family of God. Our prayer is that the fullness of the word of God is illuminated and you see that nothing is by chance. We are all a part of an eternal story.

Jonathan and Melissa Helser, Sophia, North Carolina
Songwriters and founders of the Cageless Birds and the 18 Inch Journey discipleship school

Acknowledgements

First and foremost this book is only possible because of the people who taught us the Bible and prayed we would love the story it tells: Sunday school teachers, youth leaders, spiritual mentors, wider family members, grandparents and most especially our parents. We are forever grateful for their influence in our lives and their legacy of faith which lives on in us.

Adding to these influences in the formative years of our lives it has been the close friends of our 20s and 30s with whom we discovered the treasures of the Scriptures we have woven into this book. We can't think of The God Story without the beautiful faces of these sacred companions coming to our minds. Further, our hearts are full of loving gratitude for the many precious lives who make up our local churches: Navah Church, Kansas City, and Emmanuel Church in Northern Ireland. It was in these communities The God Story was first taught, refined and formed into the content you are about to read.

All our 24-7 Prayer family who have encouraged us to get what we've preached for years into a book have been a great source of inspiration to us, embodying The God Story in radical obedience. The Vision is Jesus!

There have been numerous theologians and biblical scholars who have enriched our understanding of the Scriptures. A small number are worth mentioning for the particular way they have helped us understand the Bible: Philip Greenslade, N. T. Wright, Fleming Rutledge, Scot McKnight, Lucy Peppiatt, Lesslie Newbigin, Eugene Peterson.

We'd like to thank the team at SPCK for believing in this work and bringing it through to completion. Special heartfelt thanks to Elizabeth Neep who has helped us immensely with the editing and structure of the book and in many ways partnered with us through the shaping of The God Story.

Finally we want to thank our families. The grace they have shown as we wrote this book was immense, releasing us for hours and days on end to give ourselves to this work. In particular we want to thank our wives Rachel (Alain) and Juli (Adam). They have been our biggest supporters and champions in this endeavour, displaying strength, grace and patience in immeasurable ways.

Introduction

Two thousand years ago, two friends were walking down a dusty Middle Eastern road on the way to Emmaus when a Stranger joined them on their journey. The two travellers were living in the immediate aftermath of monumental events that would go on to define history. The Stranger recognized the friends were downcast – heads hung low and bodies slumped as they walked. Gently he drew them into conversation. Initially the friends were shocked that their fellow Traveller did not seem to know what had recently happened in their city, Jerusalem. They told the Stranger about the death of a prophet they had been following, called Jesus of Nazareth, three days earlier. As they walked and talked the Stranger became a Storyteller.

He began to tell the two friends a story they would have been familiar with but in a way they had never heard before. The Storyteller masterfully articulated how the faith of their ancestors, from beginning to end, had been fulfilled in this same Jesus whom they had followed. The two friends were enthralled by this radical retelling of a well-known story and begged their new friend to stay and share a meal with them. As the Storyteller broke the bread, the two friends recognized him as the risen Christ and then he disappeared. But their eyes had been opened and their lives would never be the same again. They reflected how their hearts had burned as they had listened to the Storyteller on the road. Immediately, they rose from the table and ran to tell their other friends what had happened: Jesus the Nazarene has risen from the dead!

This story that was shared on the Emmaus Road three days after Jesus Christ was crucified is the same story that knit our hearts together almost 20 years ago. Since then we have walked together in friendship, sharing a fascination for the story the Bible is telling, and our hearts have never stopped burning. Like the two travellers on the Emmaus Road, we've both walked through seasons of wilderness consumed with disillusionment and disappointment. And yet, even on the days when it feels like the plotline of our own lives is hanging by a thread, we've always known the faithful friendship of Jesus. He has walked alongside us in our confusion and pain, just like he did with those two travellers, asking curious and compassionate questions, gently drawing us into a more hopeful and expansive story. This book is our attempt to unravel the conversation that happened all those years ago on that dusty road.

As local pastors we long for people to be formed through the biblical narrative into confident sons and daughters of God. We have taught The God Story for many years in our churches and our prayer is that you too would step into the story which is waiting for you to play your part. We recognize that the Bible can be pretty daunting. It's one big book containing 66 smaller books of different genres and by a mixture of authors. Together these authors, each from their particular vantage point in history, are telling the story which stretches back to the beginning of time and forward into eternity. It takes them 727,969[1] words. We will try to take slightly fewer!

Our greatest prayer is that as you read this book you will be swept up in the unfolding narrative in a way that leaves you knowing both God and your own role in The God Story more. With that in mind we have imaginatively retold the biblical account of history in a way that grants the reader an appreciation for the overall trajectory of the story from one period of time to another.

As with any broad overview of history, this attempt will be limited and provisional, but our hope is that you will be 'swept up' as you learn how God has progressively unfolded his heart to humankind. You can spend the rest of your life delving into all the mystery and meaning contained in the pages of the Bible!

We also want to help you become more attuned to the sacred themes which permeate its pages, shaping the direction of the story and therefore the hearts of those who have taken it into themselves. To help you do this, we have highlighted three narrative strands that we believe knit the chapters together, uniting the entire God

Story: those of God's presence, his family and his kingdom, summarizing how these can be seen throughout various parts of the story. We've also added prayers and questions for reflection at the end of each section to be used individually or collectively.

Our great ambition is to pass on The God Story to our generation and our children's generation in the hope that its sacred themes will capture their hearts, shape their lives and catapult them right into the centre of a story still unfolding.

We pray, whether this is the first time you have heard this story or the hundredth, that your heart will burn like those of the two friends on the road to Emmaus. For that to happen you may need to invite that same Storyteller to walk with you as you read. As he began to tell those two travellers the story, he 'started at the beginning'.

Let's follow his lead as we step into The God Story together:

In the beginning . . .

1
The Origin

In the beginning God[1]

Four words introducing us to God. God before all things. Four words that pull our hearts and minds into a vortex of mesmerizing transcendence and infinite mystery.

In the beginning God . . .

Don't be fooled by the brevity. These words are the ultimate reference point for all that is, all that has been, all that will be. The God Story in all its cosmic dimensions and implications hinges on these four words. God, outside time and creation as we know it, bigger than and beyond what the human mind can fathom. We think backwards until the past vanishes and forward until our imagination collapses (or explodes!) and there is God, unchanging and undiminished in glory at both points.

In the beginning God, self-existent, outside our self-made categories, beyond what we can imagine. What in the world (or rather before the world) was God doing in the everlasting beginning? What does this even mean?

In the beginning God, the Eternal Spirit. Sheer existence. The very ground of *being*.

We don't get to make God up.

A. W. Tozer once claimed, 'What comes into your mind when you think about God is the most important thing about you.'[2] We agree. Identity. Behaviour. Purpose. Meaning. EVERYTHING flows from what we believe about God. It's *that* important. If we miss God we miss everything; if we know God we gain everything.

The God Story, before it is anything else, is God's way of telling us *who God is* and *who we are* in light of God.

So as we proceed, we invite you to open up your heart and mind. Ask the Spirit to come and draw you into a transfiguring vision of the God that this spectacular story is revealing to us.[3] Allow your heart to be moved from familiar to fascinated. What we know about God will only ever be a fraction of what there is to learn. We will spend all of eternity beholding and unfolding God. And yet, though we will never fully grasp God, he remains supremely knowable. The author of Genesis, the first book of the Bible, was convinced of this, which is why we are not presented with a scientific argument, or a flat logical description. Rather we are gifted a poem, a piece of sheer literary genius. Art is required to explain the beginning of all things, the inconceivable mystery of who God is. When it comes to Love, we need more than mere rational explanations. And of course, God the Creator is the ultimate *Lover*. God *is* love.

The Eternal Family

This God, who is not just *in the* beginning but *IS the beginning* – what can we say about him? The Hebrew word for 'God' in this opening verse is *Elohim*. *El* (singular) was an ancient generic word for 'god', as in *a divine being*. *Elohim* however is plural and implies 'divine beings'. We want to pay attention to this sense of *plurality* within the word *Elohim* in the first sentence of the Bible. The author is subtly telling us something fundamental to our understanding of God and central to God's character.

Elohim: God is *an Eternal Family*.

From the beginning, God has never been alone. To be clear, God is One. This is the great foundation of Judeo-Christian faith, and as the story unfolds we will come to see this unequivocally, so we will need to learn how to hold both of these statements – *God alone is God* and *God is not alone* – together.

Historically the church has understood God as triune. Although it took the church a while to formulate the 'doctrine' of the Trinity, the trinitarian references in Scripture have pointed many down through the ages to affirm God's *Threeness*: God the Father, God the Son, God the Holy Spirit. God is a being who is one in three and three in one. This reality of a triune God is critical for our understanding of how The God Story plot unfolds. The faint whisper revealing the Threeness of God buried in the Bible's opening refrain becomes louder and louder as the operations of the Eternal Family become more pronounced and defined in the chapters that follow.

The early theologians of the Church who helped construct this doctrine of the Trinity many years after the Bible's opening refrain was written did not merely seek to *explain* the Three-in-One God with scientific logic but attempted to teach the Church how to speak about God's mystery. They were convinced the invitation bleeding through the pages of the Bible was to view the Trinity not as a problem to solve but as a holy community of Love to fall into.

Perichoresis was the Greek word they used. This word gets at the dynamic of *mutual indwelling*. The church fathers help us contemplate how each member of the Trinity is totally yielded to the others in surrendered love.

Theologian Greg Boyd summarizes it beautifully:

As Father, Son, and Holy Spirit, God eternally exists as perfect love . . . The Father, Son, and Holy Spirit ascribe ultimate worth to one another without any competition. Their eternal life together consists in the divine joy of expressing the absolute value each has for the other.[4]

God is perfect belonging. God is love.[5]

God's love is 'other'. It is beyond human equivalent and comparison. It is unlimited in its substance and unrivalled in its purity. The biblical word for this 'otherness' is 'holy'. Contrary to what the Church throughout the ages has sometimes taught and demonstrated, God's holiness and love are not set against one another in the biblical story. Rather, God's love is revealed as the essence of his holiness.

We could say it like this: God's love is so pure, so self-giving, so undefiled, so anti-selfish that it is holy. It is incapable of hoarding or seeking self-promoting gain. God's love does not fulfil a lack within himself. God is not insecure. Free from any trace of 'self', it is impossible for God's love to manipulate, control or coerce. It can only invite and include. His holy-love therefore expresses itself as an overflowing, grace-filled intrusion into our world. It is an extraordinary invitation to share in the divine nature; to be caught up in the love of the Eternal Family.

Out of nothing comes everything

We now know before there was anything, there was God, the Eternal Family.

Now let's finish the sentence:

In the beginning God created the heavens and the earth.[6]

The God Story draws us into a wide open space, encouraging us to allow our imaginations to behold the expansive nature of God's creative expression: ultimate authority revealed in glorious beauty. 'Majesty' is the Bible's word for this. Our minds want to believe something was there *before* there was nothing. Indeed, there are countless stories, myths and legends told throughout the ancient world telling of how some kind of battle took place between 'light' and 'darkness', which 'light' eventually won. But the bold claim of the Hebrew account of creation was that there was nothing before creation – only God. This is fundamental to a Judeo-Christian creation-worldview. The Latin term used by the church fathers to express this belief is *creatio ex nihilo* (literally, 'creation out of nothing'). God was not in a contest with darkness at this point. God is over and above it and beyond it. God is in a league of his own. Out of nothing, God created everything.

The question still lingers, however: why did God create the heavens and the earth? Developing our understanding of the Trinity's self-giving, reciprocal love helps us to answer this question.

Imagine a consuming fire, a flame of passion sparking and kindling with life, exploding with energy, filled with a fiery and passionate longing to create. Creation began with a bursting forth, a joyful explosion of the Eternal Family's love.

All things were created by Love and through Love and for Love. Divine desire has birthed history and has carried it forward ever since.

Formless and empty

Now the earth was formless and empty, darkness was over the surface of the deep, and the Spirit of God was hovering over the waters. And God said . . .[7]

It's utterly thrilling to know that from the beginning God is attracted to nothingness, with the loving intention of creating something of great beauty out of it. The Hebrew words for the formless (or wild) and empty (waste) in verse 2 are the playful words, *tohu wa-bohu* (try to say it out loud!). *Tohu* means 'unordered'; *boho* means 'uninhabited'.

Over the unordered and uninhabited places of the earth the Spirit was hovering. The Spirit of God is presented to us in these early verses as wild, untameable and free. And yet, we should not understand the Spirit as some kind of random, free-floating, unseen activity at work in our world. Rather, there is an edge to this holy wind, carrying a divinely conspired and wise intention, wherever it blows. It is the very breath of God. 'Breath' and 'spirit' are the same word in the Bible. So we can say, God's own breath, the Holy Spirit, was there at the origin of all things, brooding over emptiness, ready and waiting to burst forth with goodness, beautifying the world with creativity and holy design. Think about the implications of this for a moment.

The Spirit is not hovering over the presentable places of our lives – the social media story we want everyone to see or the most glamorous versions of ourselves we parade before others. Rather he is moving over the *tohu wa-bohu* parts of our hearts, the broken and disordered parts, the empty and formless parts. Scale this up to unordered parts of our communities and uninhabited places in our nations. Here the Spirit is hovering, longing to create something more beautiful than we could ever imagine.

God is drawn to emptiness. And this is *good* news.

Chaos to order

Lots has been written on the creation account we read in Genesis 1 and 2. You'll be glad to know we are not going to go through it verse by verse or get bogged down in how literal or not this account of creation is. Such conversations often end up as adventures in missing the point. We believe that The God Story presents God's creation to us first and foremost as a divinely inspired piece of poetry, an epic and truthful description of the origin of all things, which sets the scene for the greatest love-story ever told. As Eugene Peterson reminds us, if God had simply wanted us to be concerned with inerrancy and literalism, 'he would have used the language of mathematics which is the only truly precise language we have. But of course you can't say, "I love you" in algebra.'[8]

What is clear is that into the *tohu wa-bohu*, that formless watery chaos, God came to create. The result of the creative word was a universal canvas of exuberant beauty held together in an exquisite *sacred order*.

This is not the 'order' of an authoritarian army general, a cosmic automaton or a micromanaging control freak. This is the holy design of a Creator who is a loving, free being. The One who designed it, defining it. The glorious blueprint of the ultimate Artist, Engineer and Architect. This is the genius of our Maker joyfully weaving his own beauty into the fabric of the cosmos, reflected in a multitude of sacred patterns, many of which we are still discovering in our Earth today. The 'grain of the universe'; how the Earth rotates on exactly the right axis preventing us from neither freezing to death nor being burnt to a crisp; the divine symmetry in the wings of a butterfly; the sacred swirl witnessed in spiral seeds or the cochlea of the human ear or the detail of a ram's horn. All these holy patterns are spinning and swirling through the essence of creation. This is the sacred order of the Great Designer.

The power of his voice

And God said, 'Let there be light', and there was light.[9]

The heavens and earth were not formed by any gigantic cosmic struggle of opposing forces, but simply 'by the word of the LORD'. God *spoke* and it came into being. A genesis of light and love powerfully shot out of his mouth:

By the word of the LORD the heavens were made,
their starry host by the breath of his mouth.[10]

A pattern was set in motion, the contours of which will shape many of the chapters to come: God speaks and things are called into being, 'upholding all things by the *word* of his power'.[11]

It's astonishing, pretty much inconceivable for us to imagine light shooting out of God's mouth into the expanse of the universe. But let's try to contemplate this in a spirit of wonder to appreciate better the scale of what we are trying to imagine!

We now know light travels at 300,000 km per second. If I shot a light-gun from where I am standing around the world, which is approximately 40,000 km in circumference, the light would pass through my heart seven times before it could take another beat.[12] Pretty quick, eh? Travelling at that speed I could get to the moon in one second, and in eight minutes to the sun, which is approximately 150 million km away from Earth. But if we were to travel to the edge of our galaxy, the borders of our own Milky Way, at the speed of light it would take us 50,000 years! Did you get that?! It would take 50,000 years travelling at 300,000 km per second to get to the edge of our own galaxy. Just our own galaxy. The deepest and most recent image ever created of the observable universe provides evidence of 170 billion galaxies, but a theoretical simulation predicted there could be as many as between 6 and 20 trillion.[13]

Galaxies behind galaxies behind galaxies. A universe still expanding, getting bigger every second, impossible to reach the edge of. Does your head hurt yet?

The scale of these dimensions is beyond our comprehension. Yet isn't it a joy for us to imagine, as light bursts out of the mouth of God, darkness being sent scurrying to the far reaches of the universe; the vast expanse of galaxies flooded with supernovas, black holes and more stars than there are grains of sand on the Earth?

What's more bewildering is the fact that God counts the stars and calls each one by name.[14] God's immensity must be understood in light of his intimate connection with all that God has made. It's no surprise that quantum physics has now confirmed that every single molecule within these galaxies is reverberating with sound. Imagine each atom, molecule and ion spoken into being by a loving Creator and contributing to the diverse orchestra of creation, giving praise to the One who holds it all together.

The first week of creation

As we further unfold the first week of creation, presented to us in Genesis we continue to see the voice of God as the ultimate source of power through which all that is comes into being. The literary structure of the creation account emphasizes the sacred order we have referred to above. It's an incredible piece of writing, full of divinely inspired literary genius:

- Ten acts of speaking
- Eight acts of making
- Seven pronouncements of good
- Six affirmations of: 'And God saw that it was good. And there was evening, and there was morning.'

The ten acts of speaking are split into two distinct three-day panels. In the first three days God 'separates and parts'. Light and Darkness; Day and Night; Water and Dry Land. God is ordering the unordered (*tohu*). In the next three days God 'populates and fills', inhabiting what is uninhabited (*bohu*). Life is introduced to what was lifeless. Birds fill the skies, fish swarm the seas, animals populate the land and humans inhabit the earth.

Day seven. The prose shifts. The rhythm is broken. If we look closely, we will notice the absence of the repeated refrain used to conclude the work on the previous six days, 'And there was evening, and there was morning.' On day seven we are simply told, 'so on the seventh day he [God] rested from all his work'.[15] The day is called the Sabbath or, in the Hebrew, *Shabbat*, meaning 'to stop'.

'Then God blessed the seventh day and made it holy . . .'[16]

The seventh day is different. Sabbath is supposed to look different. It is supposed to *feel* different. God introduces a sacred equilibrium to ensure a harmonious creation. Sabbath is a heavenly metronome to allow us all to keep singing in tune.

It's joyous to think of a God who delights over and celebrates what he has made. The first thing God does after he creates humankind is to rest with them and enjoy them, like a dad who looks forward to a day off with his kids. First and foremost, Sabbath should always be received as an act of Love.

The God who needs no rest is modelling something for humanity to follow. For six days, like our Maker, we are created to work, to tend to creation, to create, to populate. And then, we rest. We lay down our tools. We adore the Creator and we attend to creation.[17] Sabbath is a space to be restored and re-storied. A time for recreation and to be re-created. If we honour Sabbath-rest, everything will be better. As Walter Bruggemann concluded, 'people who keep Sabbath live all seven days differently'.[18] We would do well to recalibrate our hearts around this sacred rhythm which has been all but eliminated in twenty-first-century Western society. In our culture we need to work hard to rest well. Where the disease of consumerism threatens to kill our souls, Sabbath is our weapon of resistance.

The crown of creation

From the immense scale of 'the heavens and the earth', let's now imagine a camera lens panning in from the furthest reaches of the galaxies and sharpening its focus on one planet, then one land mass, then one garden, before freezing the frame on a tiny plot of ground. As the camera holds still, imagine what is captured. The magnificent Creator whose majestic handiwork has been written in the skies is now stooping down in the ground. This time he is not speaking creation into being but rather submerging his hands into the dirt of the ground to form a *being*:

> Then God said, 'Let us make humans in our image, according to our likeness, and let them have dominion over the fish of the sea and over the birds of the air and over the cattle and over all the wild animals of the earth and over every creeping thing that creeps upon the earth.'

> So God created humans in his own image,
>   in the image of God he created them;
>   male and female he created them.[19]

> Then the LORD God formed a man from the dust of the ground and breathed into his nostrils the breath of life, and the man became a living being.[20]

Adam, his name meaning 'earth-man', is formed. God creates Adam from dust into the most elaborate and magnificent being he has made. 'Fearfully and wonderfully' God crafts one in his own image, the details and intricacies of which we are still unable to fully understand. 'Adam' is a complex unity of muscles, neurons, cells, atoms, nerves, skin and bones and he is meticulously and delicately woven and knit together. With his own hands the Father excitedly fashions him for greatness.

Can you imagine the vested interest of the Son, the second person of the Trinity, watching with holy intrigue? Ponder him contemplating how one day he will bind himself to Adam and his descendants, in this form, forever.

After God formed Adam, he 'breathed into his nostrils the breath of life'. God gave humanity the ultimate kiss of life and Adam became *a living being*.[21] The Hebrew word for 'living being' is *nephesh* and our best English translation is 'soul'. Human beings don't have souls, they *are* souls. There is no strict separation between body and soul in the Bible. 'Soul' is not a disembodied, ethereal, floaty type of existence. 'Soul' is conscious, animated life on this earth.

Adam awakes. He opens his eyes and the first thing he sees is the most beautiful thing he will ever see: Adam is beholding glory, the source of all goodness, in the all-consuming gaze of a perfect, adoring Father. The loving connection he experiences deep in his soul is what the brain scientists of the modern world call 'secure attachment'. Face to face, Adam sees his own reflection in the loving eyes of God. His brain synapses explode and all his senses awaken simultaneously as he is overcome by the glorious wonder of Father-love. An indelible identity-mark is imprinted upon Adam's soul from the first moment he opens his eyes.

Imagine God delighting in the reflection of himself in his very own image-bearing son, like the wide-eyed wonder of a parent holding their newborn baby for the first time. God is gazing into the wonderstruck eyes of his child through whom his dream for the world, his very own nature, will be multiplied. And it fascinates him. Every person will fascinate him forever.

Original glory

The term God designates to humankind is image-bearer.[22] We were crafted from the dust into God-like beings, capable of 'imaging' and mirroring God's likeness and rule, which means before there was original sin there was *original glory*.

The Psalmist, reflecting on this glory God lavishly bestowed upon humanity, burst into his own inspired poetry years later:

what is mankind that you are mindful of them,
   human beings that you care for them?
You have made them a little lower than the angels
   and crowned them with glory and honour.
You made them rulers over the works of your hands;
   you put everything under their feet.[23]

The majestic God, who has written his glory over the heavens, has inscribed his glory on the hearts of humankind. Each one of us is laden with sacred meaning; a permanent stamp of divine nature has been imprinted upon every human being. As C. S. Lewis says, 'there are no ordinary people.'[24] No one is a *mistake*. God made you the way he likes you and likes you the way he made you. You are God's unique and unrepeatable idea. His eyes saw your unformed substance in your mother's womb. Every day of your life has been packed with potential to reflect the glory of your Creator.

Life in the garden

Now the LORD God had planted a garden in the east, in Eden;
and there he put the man he had formed.[25]

After God made humankind he created a home for his sons and daughters called the Garden of Eden. Through the first chapters of The God Story we begin to witness humankind outwork their original glory in the garden. Further, we are able to recognize three distinct elements of their image-bearing likeness. These three ways – (1) relationship with God, (2) relationship to one another and (3) relationship to creation – help reveal the God-designed identity and vocation intended for humankind.

Relationship with God

From the opening pages of The God Story, it is clear that human-kind's original glory was to be defined by reciprocal intimate, free-flowing communion with God. The delightful imagery of God walking with man in the cool of the day[26] provides clear and beautiful evidence for this. Eden, God's original home for humankind, means 'pleasure' or 'paradise'. Humankind was created to experience the pleasure and presence of the Father. The plotline is built upon God's burning desire for friendship. We were born to walk with God. We were created to be with the Great Lover of our souls. One with our Maker. We see this friendship is to be received as a gift. God did not make robots! He could never force humankind to love him or it wouldn't be perfect love. God's holy love speaks of ultimate freedom. God was not laying down a demand to love him in the creation of humanity, rather he was carrying a hope in his heart, a hope that we would freely return the love he has for us.

The particular ways God longed for humanity to drink in this perfect cocktail of love and freedom were expressed in the way he designed the Garden of Eden. Humankind were given permission to enjoy the delights of the garden where they would feast on the pleasures of the Father, expressing their wholehearted trust in his heart and provision for them. Two trees in particular are given prominence in the narrative: the Tree of Life and the Tree of the Knowledge of Good and Evil. The Tree of Life symbolized God's desire for humankind to find their life in God and live their life with God. Feasting on this tree would deepen their understanding of their true identity as fully dependent sons and daughters of God. The Tree of the Knowledge of Good and Evil symbolized humankind's pride and independence to do what seems right in their own eyes. They were never meant to live life apart from God. This helps us understand the one prohibition God gave Adam and Eve: 'you must not eat from the tree of the knowledge of good and evil.'[27] As all good parents establish boundaries to enable life to flourish because they love their children and seek their best, here we witness the perfect Father set loving terms for his relationship with humankind. These guardrails allowed room for exquisite wonder, exhilarating freedom and the protection from harm.

Was granting this level of freedom a risk? Absolutely! The gift of free will meant these terms could be resisted. The loving freedom that characterized our original glory carried an unthinkable implication: God faced the possibility of being caught up in a drama of rejection.

So why did God do it? Quite simply, it appears we were worth the risk. Or as Chris Green concludes beautifully, 'God would rather not be God at all than be God without us.'[28] The sheer delight of loving us and the hope we might love him in return were too much for God to resist. The question is, and has long been, will humankind freely offer back to God the love that birthed them in the first place?

Relationship to one another

The second distinct element of humankind's original glory becomes clear through the first 'not good' in the Bible. Remember, everything has been good to this point. 'Not good' is supposed to grab our attention.

> The LORD God said, 'It is not good for the man to be alone. I will make a helper suitable for him.'[29]

Why is it 'not good' for the man to be alone? Because God *is not alone*. Aloneness is not part of the original glory. We were created for family, designed for friendship.

Adam needs a suitable companion and God has a surprise up his sleeve, the great crescendo to all of creation. The Genesis 2 account reveals Adam undertaking his first image-bearing assignment: the naming of all the animals. After what must have been a thrilling day, Adam experiences something of an anticlimax. Despite the magnificence of the vast array of creatures in front of him and the exhilaration he would have enjoyed as he designated titles to each of them, he has failed to discover a true companion, one like him. We imagine God brimming with joy as he watches his son stewarding God's creatures with dignity and honour, and then a cheeky smile begin to break out on the Father's face as Adam's excitement turns to frustration and loneliness. The Eternal Family has kept the best until the last for his beloved son.

The Father puts Adam into a deep sleep. A rib is removed from Adam's side and once again we imagine God stooping down to form and create. The result is a masterpiece. God's image is uniquely revealed in a woman. Like a dress rehearsal for the countless wedding days that would take place down through the ages, the Father walks his exquisite daughter, Eve, to his waiting son. Adam awakes and, as he gazes on her beauty, he responds with an exuberant explosion of joy: 'bone of my bones and flesh of my flesh'.[30] Eve is the perfect mixture of authority, strength and durability (bone) and vulnerability, compassion and tenderness (flesh).[31]

Adam and Eve will become 'one flesh'.[32] This oneness which humankind is given to enjoy is to be understood as a reflection of the oneness God himself is: an Eternal Family so in love with one another that they are One! Male and female, both made in the image of God, living in peaceful coexistence. No hierarchy, no domination, no control; only free-flowing, self-giving love, mutual honour and companionship. Unity in diversity. Distinct beings joined in a community capable of experiencing a transcendent oneness and the ability to produce life.

The oneness of Adam and Eve is an obvious archetype for how the Church has understood marriage for centuries. But this account is also a wider reflection of the Eternal Family's desire for an extended family on the earth. God's very nature is an interdependent relationship so he is best reflected in the context of community. As image-bearers, we are only fully human in relationship, in friendship, in family.

The original glory of Eden reveals, as we surrender our hearts to God in free-flowing love, that we are designed to mimic the Trinity through self-giving love to one another. We are loved by a Father and we are formed in a family. Fellow human beings should be understood primarily as gifts to one another, each one capable of reflecting an unrepeatable dimension of the image of God to the other.

Relationship to creation

It's obvious God *enjoyed* Eden. More, he delighted in the reality of his image-bearing sons and daughters enjoying its pleasure. Eden was the quintessential 'thin place', a term used to describe a place where the distance between heaven and earth is so thin they have become one.

It is clear the Garden of Eden was a physical place,[33] a specific plot of land, and its location was circumscribed by geographical markers.[34] This is important because it reveals something crucial about the divine vocation delegated to Adam and Eve in the beginning. God had a job for Adam and Eve to do not just in Eden *but beyond Eden too*:

> God blessed them and said to them, 'Be fruitful and increase in number; fill the earth and subdue it. Rule over the fish in the sea and the birds in the sky and over every living creature that moves on the ground.'[35]

The original glory of humankind's vocation involved nothing less than the expanding of the borders of Eden throughout the whole earth, multiplying the blessing of God and extending his loving reign. Adam and Eve, as God's vice-regents and trusted rulers, were delegated authority to work on God's behalf, co-creating in relationship with God for the flourishing of creation.

God supplied all the raw materials but placed divine responsibility on humankind to steward and create according to God's design and instruction in a way that both deeply satisfies our souls and reflects back to God his own glory. This is the work of our hands as human beings. 'Work' was part of the image-bearing glory *before sin*. We are called to co-create the culture of Eden with our heavenly Father in all of life. From business to botany, politics to performing arts, carpentry to quantum physics. God wants the culture of heaven established throughout the earth.

As we conclude this opening chapter, in which many beautiful and profound themes have been woven together to describe the

Origin of all things, let's allow the Spirit to draw us into the holy mystery at the heart of The God Story.

The breath of God has birthed time and space. Divine desire will carry history forward from this point. Love's greatest longing has been satisfied. The Eternal Family's dream has been realized.

God is with Adam and Eve. They are with God.

Everything is right in the world.

This is home.

Presence: In the beginning God is love. Overflowing divine desire created beauty out of nothing. The crown of God's creation was human beings, those who bore God's image. God has a burning desire for friendship with humankind. He did not need our love but he wanted to be known. God walked with Adam and Eve 'in the cool of the day', enjoying intimate friendship. Eden was pure pleasure. God's intention was that we would live in free-flowing communion with him forever. This is our original design.

Family: God is an Eternal Family, a loving community of joy, honour and mutual submission. In creation God was opening up this community to include humankind. This is the home life of God each one of us has been invited into. As image-bearers we were created to live together as a reflection of the Eternal Family.

Kingdom: God created a world to be filled with his loving reign and rule, as a reflection of his own glory and beauty. Those made in his image were formed to co-create with God in extending the paradise of Eden, the culture of heaven, throughout the earth.

Father, we pray you would help us to know more of your passionate desire to commune with us. Help us to grow in friendship with you, to walk with you 'in the cool of the day'. We want to be formed in the love of the Eternal Family so we can participate with you in your dream for the world. We want to rediscover what it is to co-create with you to bring about your kingdom throughout the earth.

Questions for reflection: What did you discover about God, people and the world in this part of the story? How does it make you feel to know you have been invited into the love of the Eternal Family? How does understanding the three elements of your original design (relationship with God; relationship with others; stewarding creation) help you understand God's call upon your life?

2

The Fall

Four words explained the origins of The God Story and helped establish its essential plotline. Now six words point towards a tragic turn in the plot:

Now the serpent was more crafty . . .[1]

The Story is off to a perfect start. Then, a severe jolt takes place. No one really knows how long God and humankind enjoyed the beauty of Eden together. What we are told, though, is that another character has been introduced, offering a calculated threat. Interestingly, The God Story doesn't give us an answer for how the serpent got into God's perfect garden, but what it does clearly present is an archetypal personification of evil. We are left not to rationalize the source of evil but to be sure evil has an *identity*. The Fall narrative sets the scene for the unfolding drama of resistance woven through the rest of The God Story and the incalculable level of devastation that is to follow.

Battle lines have been drawn. A war has been launched. From this point on everything will be contested.

This serpent is described as 'crafty'. The Hebrew word for this, *arum*, gets at the idea of 'a negative use of intelligence' or 'a perversion of wisdom'. We should take note. The adversary is not, as commonly portrayed, an ugly little red devil running around with a pitchfork, spitting fire. Rather, in his first appearance in The God Story he is presented as a nefarious crafty imposter corrupting and perverting God's truth.

At this point we need some help from two other parts of the Bible to fill out our understanding of the figure this serpent represents. Passages in Ezekiel and Isaiah help paint a picture of a heavenly angel once part of God's divine council who became enamoured with his own brilliance, so much so he arrogantly described himself 'above the stars of God'.[2] His self-deception fuelled a jealousy against God and his intentions for humankind which ultimately led to an outright rebellion among God's divine council. The enemy was expelled, and a host of rogue angels followed the prince of pride out of God's presence, seeking to resist God's purposes ever since. The biblical word for this enemy is 'the Satan', which is a Hebrew word meaning 'adversary'.

Crafty serpent

Before we learn more about the catastrophic role the serpent plays in Genesis, we need to remind ourselves of the one prohibition God gave to humankind, and in doing so re-emphasize how much was at stake:

> And the LORD God commanded the man, 'You are free to eat from any tree in the garden; but you must not eat from the tree of the knowledge of good and evil, for when you eat from it you will certainly die.'[3]

As we have established in Chapter 1, the Tree of Life symbolized God's desire for Adam and Eve to find their loving dependency and secure identity in God alone. The Tree of the Knowledge of Good and Evil was the forbidden tree at the centre of the garden. Why would God not want Adam and Eve to possess this knowledge? What was so terrible about it? Well, first and foremost they didn't need it. God had created them to be perfectly fulfilled in God's unbounded love. Second, the idea of 'knowledge' in this context was an attempt by humans to define and experience good and evil on their own. In other words, eating of this tree would symbolize an act of outright independence, a desire for wisdom apart from God, and a violation of their wholehearted union with God.

It is into this context the serpent comes:

He said to the woman, 'Did God really say, "You must not eat from any tree in the garden"?'

The woman said to the serpent, 'We may eat fruit from the trees in the garden, but God did say, "You must not eat fruit from the tree that is in the middle of the garden, and you must not touch it, or you will die."'

'You will not certainly die,' the serpent said to the woman. 'For God knows that when you eat from it your eyes will be opened, and you will be like God, knowing good and evil.'[4]

As we read this verse carefully we become aware of the insidious ways the crafty serpent asserted his influence in Eden. Two main tactics become apparent, evil strategies he has consistently deployed against humanity down through the ages.

Distorting who God is

Remember those words of Tozer, 'What comes into your mind when you think about God is the most important thing about you'? The enemy is smart enough to know this truth and therefore launches an all-out attack on the image-bearers' minds, seeding doubt concerning God's word to them and distorting the sound of the Father's loving, identity-forming voice in their souls. The serpent's actions reveal Satan is not primarily interested in getting us to deny the existence of God as much as he is in twisting our understanding of God. Satan will make claims about God's truth, yet presents them in false ways, cleverly using God's word against us. *Did God really say, you must not eat from any tree in the garden?*

Can you see how Satan is posturing God's word towards Adam and Eve in a deceitful way, causing them to question God's goodness? Can you see the lie that is being spun in the image-bearers' minds: 'Maybe God cannot be fully trusted, maybe he wants to control us more than love us, maybe God is keeping something from us, maybe we need to do more than simply trust his word?'

Distorting who we are

The serpent knew if he could twist who God is in the mind of the image-bearers he could twist how they understood their identity in light of him. Genesis 3 is the most devastating account of identity theft you will ever read. Here we witness the enemy steal the core of humankind's identity in the tender place of their belonging. Adam and Eve were already made in the image and likeness of God. The luring voice of the serpent deceived them into believing there was something more they needed to do. It was the voice that says 'know more', 'achieve more', 'become more'. It was the voice that says, 'Don't settle for being like God, you can be God!' The serpent's tactics help us realize the enemy's trickery is built upon the seductive irony of making us believe he is actually giving us identity: 'your eyes will be opened, and you will be like God'.[5] But tragically, once we begin to believe that the goodness of God is not enough for us, it won't be long before we start to believe that we are not enough.

The Fall narrative reveals the serpent's tactic was aimed at a much more devastating consequence than simply getting Adam and Eve to 'break the rules'. His 'crafty' voice seduced them to forfeit their beloved identity. Satan we learn is the ultimate thief, a manipulator par excellence, a murderer from the beginning.

Taking the bait

When the woman saw that the fruit of the tree was good for food and pleasing to the eye, and also desirable for gaining wisdom, she took some and ate it. She also gave some to her husband, who was with her, and he ate it.[6]

There is no easy way to say it. Adam and Eve ate the forbidden fruit. As they bit down into the fruit, something broke within the heart of God. Longing love once satisfied is now filled with ache. God began to grieve a loss of intimacy with Adam and Eve. Further, a deadly poison infected humankind from this point on. No one can possibly fathom the incalculable pain and collateral damage that would ripple down through human history from this one, seemingly small, disobedient act.

What will happen next? Remember the consequence of God's one prohibition, 'You must not eat it, or you will die.' Will God let them die immediately? Will he sever his tie to them, leaving them to their own meaningless existence? No! Remarkably, God goes looking for Adam and Eve. The plotline may be convulsing with the tragic consequences of their disobedience but it is also at the same time revealing God can't stand the distance.

The Father's desire for intimate friendship and communion has been shattered and his original dream for humanity dismantled, but his undiminished love will not abandon his image-bearers. Instead, God is already searching for his son and daughter in the hope they will still walk with him. This consuming desire in the heart of God is now achingly expressed in his piercing question to Adam and Eve:

Where are you?[7]

Feel the emotion in God's voice as he winces with purified pain, mourning the loss of his own dream. This is the first time in The God Story, but certainly not the last, we are given a glimpse into the anguished heart of God. Yet the question, 'Where are you?' emphatically confirms God will not turn his back on his son and daughter. Incredibly he has already started to look for them. Adam and Eve will run but they can't hide. Neither can we. God comes looking, relentlessly, in love. And the echo of God's question to Adam and Eve, 'Where are you?' resounds with the tone of pursuing love on every subsequent page of The God Story. *Where have you gone? I miss you . . .*

The great pursuit for lost sons and daughters has begun. God will keep coming for his image-bearers. *God can't stand the distance.*

Fear, shame and the Blame Game

Things aren't going to be the same for a while, though. As we read on through the Fall narrative we discover Adam and Eve immediately recognizing that something has changed. Tragically it appears they became aware of a radical diminishment in their identity. Their once innocent and captivating view of the world has now been corrupted into a chaotic and distorted reality field. Everything appears different now: God, themselves, the world. In particular, Adam and Eve experience two new psychological realities that will become the perennial archenemies of the human soul.

Shame and fear.

> Then the eyes of both of them were opened, and they realized they were naked; so they sewed fig leaves together and made coverings for themselves.[8]

Adam and Eve begin to notice that sick feeling in their stomachs we have all experienced when we realize we have done something we never thought we would do. That jarring loss of innocence we suffer after we have compromised truth for popularity or substituted God's love for a momentary pleasure.

We are told their 'eyes . . . were opened', not in a good way. Adam and Eve no longer feel who God says they are is *enough*. Innocence has been lost as shame begins to seep into their souls. They begin to experience that inward-looking glare of condemnation, failure and self-criticism many of us have become all too familiar with. Shame, we learn in this narrative, runs deeper than guilt. Guilt is the bad feeling we experience in response to a specific mistake we have made. Shame is the all-consuming negative feeling about who we are. Further, as this account reveals, wherever shame manifests itself we can be sure its shadowy partner 'fear' isn't too far away:

> I heard you in the garden, and I was afraid because I was naked; so I hid.[9]

'I was afraid,' Adam declares, when God comes looking for him. The distance Adam and Eve's disobedience creates is a tangible reality. Shame causes them to feel unworthy of connection and fear pounces on the opportunity the distance creates. Shame distorts how Adam and Eve feel about themselves. Fear distorts how they understand God. Adam and Eve realize they don't know God like they once did, and in the dreadful exposure of being separated from the source of love, fear becomes their new way of apprehending reality. Fear exists in the absence of God's securing love. Distanced from the Love that always wants the best for us, an anxious panicked belief that we must control the uncontrollable sets in. Like Adam and Eve, we find ourselves haunted by a new set of questions we were originally designed to never have to ask: What will God do to us now? Does he still love us? Does he really want the best for us?

Satan and his demons have continually drip-fed these defeating influences – shame and fear – into the minds of cracked image-bearers for centuries. He uses fear and shame to intimidate us so that they become intimacy barriers, stopping us from making it back into the original communion we were born to know with God. Think about it for a minute. Reflect on any dysfunctional pattern in your life and we can almost certainly predict you will find a stem of fear or shame trying to choke you in the midst of it. Together they form a demonic tag-team, constituting Satan's most prized artillery in his resistance to the purposes of God through humankind on the earth. Exposing these schemes of the crafty serpent helps explain why one of the other names The God Story uses to describe him is 'devil'. The root of 'devil' (*diabolos*) points us more literally to the idea of 'slanderer' or 'accuser'. As the narrative unfolds we will witness this adversary of our souls constantly reminding image-bearers of their past mistakes and their current weaknesses.

In order to deal with these overwhelming feelings of shame and fear, Adam and Eve learned how to hide and cover themselves: 'they sewed fig leaves together and made coverings for themselves.'[10] Human beings have been following suit ever since. As well as the more obvious destructive patterns of self-medicating, suicide and self-harming, we deal with shame in more subconscious, subtle, everyday ways. Our posturing to be noticed, our obsession with 'likes', 'views' and new 'followers', our pursuit of success, our outward attempts to appear holy, every day we cover ourselves with clothes from our own 'fig-leaf' wardrobes, seeking to prove ourselves worthy and earn a love that was always ours in the first place. In short, we become skilled in self-protecting *and* self-projecting to cover up and hide how we really feel about ourselves.

The other way humankind deals with shame and fear is through what we call the 'Blame Game'. As we read the next two verses, in response to God's direct questions, we witness a succession of blaming coupled with a defensive abdication of responsibility.

First Adam places blame on Eve and God for his and Eve's disobedient act:

The woman you put here with me – she gave me some fruit from the tree, and I ate it.[11]

Then Eve blames the serpent:

The serpent deceived me, and I ate.[12]

These reactions from both Adam and Eve reinforce what we are coming to understand about ourselves – we cannot bear the feeling of not being enough. Scrambling for some way to soothe this dreaded feeling, we self-protect to deflect shame. Blaming someone or something else feels like the quickest and easiest way out. We find ways, often elaborate yet always deceitful, to divert responsibility for our actions on to 'the other'. Every parent attempting to correct their child knows this game all too well. Yet from the playground row to the complex dynamics of the highest political offices, the pervasive Blame Game sucks everyone in.

Fear, shame and the Blame Game – these intrusions into God's good world dictate the drama of our everyday lives as we clamber to present the best versions of ourselves. Yet we must take note – these versions are not our true selves. They are illusions influenced by the father of lies[13] himself.

Now that we know this, we don't have to believe them.

The disease of sin

From the moment Adam and Eve bit into the forbidden fruit, sin infected the human heart, and like a self-destructing virus, it began to do untold damage to the image-bearing design. We know an enemy exists outside humankind (Satan), but now the story has introduced a new foe conceived *within* humankind. From this point on a powerful damaging force resident within the human heart will seek to master the body and the soul, enticing it to serve its own desires. The Bible will later define this force as 'the flesh' – our base nature which strives for self-gratification. We have become kings and queens of our own hearts, the centre of our own story.

Sin, we can conclude, is not merely the 'bad things' we do but an unrelenting force of independence which seeks to shape us in our inward being. The primacy of our own will, reinforced by culture's relentless pounding of the industry of 'self', is too strong for us to control. The Psalmist, in a moment of sober awareness of his brutish innate selfishness, confessed, 'Behold, I was shapen in iniquity; and in sin did my mother conceive me.'[14] Hundreds of years later Saint Augustine would concur, 'Without you, what am I to myself but a guide to my own self-destruction.'[15]

Ultimately humanity can't be fully trusted, and needs to be saved from its own personal drama, for 'the curvature in the crooked human heart . . . always bends back on itself.'[16]

Consequences

The consequences of Adam and Eve's act of disobedience are far reaching. The complete reversal of the original blessing mandate ('God blessed them. And God said to them, "Be fruitful and multiply"'[17]) began to take place. Sin rather than blessing multiplies. Where there was once only the fragrance of flourishing there is only the putrefying stench of decay as the whole of creation is infected by sin. The three main elements of humankind's original glory are tragically impacted: humankind's relationships with God, one another and creation are ruptured and broken.

We have already alluded to the consequences of distance between God and humankind and the consequences of division between man and woman. But the text goes on to reveal further consequences, determined by God, which impact the whole of the created order. Ultimately, as God said it would, death has entered the world. Adam and Eve will one day return to the dust. For now man will have to strive with the ground. What was originally a strife-free glorious mission will turn into days of opposition and bleak drudgery. Women will experience the excruciating pain of childbearing. The curse of sin will trickle into the earth and work itself through the fabric of creation.

God knows that once human beings choose to redefine good and evil they have the potential to become beastly themselves, not unlike the serpent who deceived them. Woefully, God knows Adam and Eve will now be more enamoured with their own reflection than with the peerless beauty of his face, the original source of all their delight and purpose. Pride cannot survive in the manifest presence of God. It has to go.

Adam and Eve now have to leave Eden.

Glimmers of grace

The chances are you may have been taught to only notice God's judgement and displeasure with Adam and Eve at this point in The God Story. But when we look more closely, we see beautiful glimmers of grace.

First, God preserves humankind. When all the conditions pointed to death, God still blesses humankind with life. We should become aware of how God, despite his anguished heart, is unable to let go of his disobedient sons and daughters, pursuing them even in their shame and hiding. While the task has become monumentally more difficult, Adam and Eve can still have a part to play in the stewardship of creation.

Second, he covers up mankind's shame: 'The LORD God made garments of skin for Adam and his wife and clothed them.'[18] We have identified how Adam and Eve sought to hide from God and cover up their shame. Yet a few verses later we are awed by the mercy of a loving God who longs to tenderly dress them. Incredibly, it appears God is deeply troubled by the reality of his children enduring shame, self-hatred and the dread of feeling exposed. God chooses to cover their sin and shame with a handmade design of sacrificial animal skins. In this moving and beautiful paternal act God is effectively communicating to his children, *I am still here for you; where you can't cover your nakedness and shame, I will cover you.*

Third, in the middle of his righteous and forthright rebuke to Adam and Eve, God also confronts the serpent, saying:

> And I will put enmity
>   between you and the woman,
>   and between your offspring and hers;
> he will crush your head,
>   and you will strike [or bruise] his heel.[19]

Humanity will endure the results of their rebellion, but a hopeful thread has already started to be woven – one of Eve's offspring will one day deal with this curse decisively, eventually crushing the evil serpent's head. God may be lamenting his dream but he is not feeling sorry for himself. Plans have been made and a divine strategy has been conceived. The cost will be a 'bruising' unlike anything the world has ever seen, yet the rescue mission has begun. The serpent will not have the last word.

All is not lost.

The journey east

> After he drove the man out, he placed on the east side of the Garden of Eden cherubim and a flaming sword flashing back and forth to guard the way to the tree of life.[20]

The phrase 'east of Eden' will become the unfortunate moniker for humankind's movement away from their original homeland, the presence of God. Tragically, the fruit of Adam and Eve's sin doesn't slowly ripen but quickly matures in the next generation. Cain, their eldest son, calls his younger brother Abel to meet him in a field one day and murders him. Humankind is already moving further east.

> So Cain went out from the LORD's presence and lived in the land of Nod, east of Eden.[21]

This is such a gut-wrenching phrase. Eugene Peterson translates 'east of Eden', 'No-Man's-Land'.[22] Devastating! Yet the narrative reveals that despite Cain's rebellion God placed a mark of protection on him.[23] Yet another undeserved glimmer of grace. Like his father Adam, though, Cain will have to face disastrous consequences. The mark he bears will release seven-fold vengeance.[24] As Cain travels further east from the unbroken presence of God he takes human society with him.

Cain will eventually build a city founded on the principle of 'protection' from the other. Civilization will be built upon the false and distorted dualism of 'us vs them'. This is the Blame Game on steroids – cities and nations established on the lie that the 'other' is against us and the even stronger lie that only violence can protect us. Siblings will turn against siblings, children against parents, nation against nation. At this point, The God Story is teaching us that when individuals, motivated by sin, join together in causes contrary to God's original purpose, systems of sin are established, expressed in destructive collective patterns of injustice, greed, racism, slavery and abuse, particularly the abuse of women. As subsequent generations are recorded in the next few chapters, powerful cycles of sin will spin wildly out of control.[25] We are faced with the stark reality of the dramatic descent into violence and devastation the Fall has brought about.

The Flood

As we reach Genesis chapter 6, The God Story cannot disguise how bad things really get. As the narrative describes the extremes of the cosmic rebellion taking place in the heavens and the earth, we come to two devastating verses:

> The LORD saw how great the wickedness of the human race had become on the earth, and that every inclination of the thoughts of the human heart was only evil all the time. The LORD regretted that he had made human beings on the earth, and his heart was deeply troubled.[26]

At this point in the story God is only experiencing pain, grief and regret. God's creation is repulsing him so much, God is 'sorry' he made the earth. Can you even begin to imagine what this must have felt like for God?

God knows something must be done. The transgression is so great, the wicked rebellion in man's heart so pronounced and the covenantal promise so utterly rejected by his sons and daughters that in great sorrow God allows creation to be washed away. God floods the earth, allowing the world to dissolve back into its original state of chaos, in order that it might be re-created all over again.

The Flood is an expression of God's righteous anger, often referred to in the Bible as his 'wrath' – a recurring theme in The God Story. The Flood may be the lowest point of the story to date but what we actually come to recognize, if we read this text carefully, is not an angry God but a grieving parent deeply involved in the life of his creation. The flood waters may have broken open dams, but a much greater brokenness is taking place in the heart of God. The Hebrew word used in the verse above (verse 6) to describe God's grief is the same word used back in Genesis 3.16 to describe the pain Eve would experience in childbirth. Ponder this for a moment. God, like the agony of a woman in full-blown labour, is aching, crying out with excruciating pain from a place of deep distress, but, remarkably, this process of pain also contains a promise of a new beginning. God's righteous anger flows out of a broken heart filled with perfect love as it meets sin and injustice. His love is not passive or negligible but active, purifying and restorative, always carrying the possibility of bringing to birth a fresh alternative.

Noah is a man who offers hope for that fresh alternative. 'Noah was a righteous man, blameless among the people of his time, and he walked faithfully with God.'[27] Noah obediently builds an ark for his family and takes with him a sampling of creation. Imagine Noah's faithful obedience, day after day, decade after decade, preparing an ark based on an unprecedented word from God and a promise that he and all the inhabitants of the ark will survive the coming flood.

As Noah comes out of the Ark after 40 days of rain he is presented to us as a type of new Adam carrying the same original commission. Check out how the words are almost identical to those that were given to Adam and Eve: 'Be fruitful and increase in number and fill the earth.'[28] God is re-establishing his original dream to have an extended family on the earth. To prove this, God reaffirms his vows to humankind, declaring how he is covenantally bound to it forever. Further, he declares he will never allow a flood like this to happen on the earth again. To symbolize the sealing of God's vows to humankind he lights up the sky with a rainbow. From ground-zero perspective we see a rainbow as a bow-shaped half-circle resting on the horizon, but from the vantage point of the sky (ask any pilot!) a rainbow can be seen for what it truly is: an *unending full circle* of iridescent colour and radiance. Think of a rainbow as a kind of multicoloured wedding ring, the sign of God's unfailing commitment to his creation painted in the sky, an emblem of his covenant and the promise of his presence. Remarkably, we are told a rainbow is also a reminder to God's own heart of his promise. Every time he hangs one in the sky we can imagine a conversation among the Trinity: 'That was too painful, we can never do that again, we love this creation – broken and rebellious and all it may be – way too much.'

Babel

Despite the attempted reboot of creation, after the Flood another cycle of sin begins. Notice the pattern. God blesses Noah. Noah plants a garden. Noah sins in the garden. His sons divide as a result of his sin. The cycle then multiplies exponentially, through Noah's generational line.

Generations later The God Story tells us Noah's descendants gathered in a valley to build a city and a tower. This city was founded on the self-promoting principle, 'let us . . . make a name for ourselves'.[29] The serpent's deceptive whisper in Eden, 'You can be like God,' had reverberated around the earth for generations, culminating in this collective insurrection against God. Humankind had forfeited its original vocation to steward God's blessing and instead built a monument unto themselves.

The Tower of Babel serves as a graphic reminder of where things will end up when humankind chooses to walk its own self-determined path. Babel is a precursor to the regime of Babylon. Babylon, as we will confirm in later chapters, is the Bible's paradigmatic anti-Edenic state of existence; it carries the image of an empire architected around human power working in opposition to the loving reign of God on the earth. This type of self-serving regime promotes a way of civilization built on independence and alienation from divine love and relationship. Those who have sold out to such an empire are really pledging allegiance to their own fantasies of greatness, worshipping a projection of their own desires. Only God knows how catastrophic this unified attempt to attain greatness apart from him will be. He promised not to flood the earth again but he has to do something to stop humankind from the cataclysmic consequences of their rebellion. This time God chooses to scatter the people, sending them off literally babbling in different languages.[30]

This thoroughly depressing scene is in some ways an appropriate ending to the opening prologue of The God Story (Genesis 1—11). In one way it seems the story is becoming predictable – humankind can't be trusted to make the world a better place through their own efforts. The influence of the crafty serpent (the devil) has become pronounced throughout the story, distorting humanity's view of God and themselves, ensnaring them in chains of fear and shame. The disease of self-gratification (the flesh), which infected the human heart through Adam and Eve's disobedience, has spread throughout the earth, proving itself as an uncontrollable destructive force within humankind. Cycles of sin have multiplied throughout Adam's descendants to produce systems of collective sinfulness (the world). Operating under Satan and his rebellious kingdom's control, humankind has completely failed to fulfil the original mandate. Generation after generation have moved further east of Eden, away from their true home.

Like a faithful parent, broken-hearted by their children's constant disobedience and wilful rebellion but knowing the only way to win them back long term is to lovingly release them, God has let the nations of the earth go their separate ways.

But make no mistake. Divine desire has not been diminished. Longing love has not given up. Just as God came looking in the garden, God will keep searching for the ones he loves. God may have scattered the nations, but within this dispersing there is a plan. A rescue mission to redeem, renew and restore his fallen creation. God will narrow the focus on a particular people with the hope that through them God's eternal purpose to woo all nations back to himself will come to pass.

The question is: will God find a suitable partner, a people who will carry his name?

Presence: God's heart has been broken by Adam and Eve's disobedience. The communion God wanted to enjoy with humanity has been drastically and devastatingly impacted. Adam and Eve will walk out of Eden. Yet God can't stand the distance. He will pursue his lost sons and daughters in the hope they will return to this place of friendship with him. From this point on, God's cry to Adam and Eve, 'Where are you?' will echo throughout history. Despite our sin, God still wants us.

Family: The effects of humankind's sin had catastrophic consequences for their relationships with one another. God's dream for a family reflecting his nature on the earth looks to be in tatters. In stealing our identity, the enemy has turned us against one another; the Blame Game has begun. Comparison, jealousy, division and war result.

Kingdom: A dark and opposing force, the Satan, has entered the story. From this point on the kingdom of darkness will contest the plans and purposes of God in the world. Tragically, rather than fulfilling their original glory of extending the loving reign of God, humankind have only sought to build their own kingdoms: Adam and Eve. Cain. Humankind before the Flood. Babel. Disconnected from the true Source of our lives, humankind will do untold damage to creation rather than steward it gloriously.

Father, we recognize our sin breaks your heart as you watch us damage ourselves, one another and the world you created for us to steward. Our hearts are moved, though, as we realize you can't stand the distance. We hear you cry out to us, 'Where are you?' We repent of our sin, Father. Help us to reject the deceptions of the enemy – fear and shame and the Blame Game – and come home to your love.

Questions for reflection: Is there anything causing you to hide from God in fear or to cover yourself because of shame? Sin ruins relationships. Is there any relationship you have that needs to be reconciled? What steps can you take now towards that end?

3

The Seed of Promise

Abram's introduction to The God Story is a startling moment which shatters the hollow and nebulous tone Genesis 11 has ended with. We cannot pay close enough attention to the sacred interaction we are about to explore. This hinge point in history is the moment the Bible will spend the rest of its pages unfolding.

Seemingly out of nowhere, God comes to Abram and speaks. God tells Abram to leave his home and start walking into a new and unknown frontier:

> The LORD had said to Abram, 'Go from your country, your people and your father's household to the land I will show you.'[1]

God calls Abram to detach himself, layer after layer, in progressive vulnerability, from all that is familiar to his heart: his country, his people, his family. It seems wholesale relinquishment of all other loves is the prerequisite to walking fully in friendship with God.

Why would Abram leave? Why would he embark on this epic pilgrimage, from the known to the unknown? What could trigger such holy wanderlust in these ageing years of his life?

The promise and the Voice

Ultimately, we must conclude there was something about *the Voice*. A Voice so compelling, so intriguing, Abram simply couldn't resist it. A Voice not coercive but evocative, not compulsory but inviting. The captivating cadence carried in this Voice, the same desiring

Voice that had soothed the souls of Adam and Eve in Eden, appears to have touched a nerve in Abram's tired soul, calling him out of a life of mediocre existence and into an adventure he had never imagined. This was the Voice of holy disruption. A Voice carrying promise.

> I will make you into a great nation,
>   and I will bless you;
> I will make your name great,
>   and you will be a blessing.
> I will bless those who bless you,
>   and whoever curses you I will curse;
> and all peoples on earth
>   will be blessed through you.[2]

It's bewildering yet delightful to think that the God of the universe called a wandering farmer, with nothing but an available heart, out of his own little story into a plot that would change the destiny of all the nations on earth.

Let's ponder this for a second. How would you react if you heard the Creator of the universe making a promise that all the families on earth would be blessed through your ordinary, seemingly insignificant life and family?

The promise God gave to Abram was a reformulation of the original blessing in Eden. The continuity with Adam and Noah is obvious. The same God who has desired humanity from the beginning still longs for his image-bearers to truly fulfil their destiny as his co-partners. The call is 'reformulated' because, against the backdrop of the ongoing rebellion of the nations we described in the previous chapter, a distinctive element to Abram's calling has been introduced. God has narrowed the focus. God is choosing a particular group of people as his own, with the hope of fashioning them into an alternative community reflecting his nature and calling all nations back to his heart. What is sometimes known as the 'scandal of particularity' (choosing one specific people group) was always for ultimate inclusivity (in the end to have all nations). God still longs to fill the whole earth with his loving presence and glory, but the 'means' God is using is now more distinct. A seed of universal blessing carrying within it an expanse of hope which will stretch to all mankind is being planted in Abram's heart, testing his trust to the very end. Nothing less than a plan for global redemption is being conceived in the heart of this ordinary nomad. Abram and his family have been blessed to be a blessing to all.

Notice the details at the end of chapter 11 which reveal Abram's original homeland: Mesopotamia, or 'Ur of the Chaldeans' to put it precisely. This is much more significant than people usually realize. Ur of the Chaldeans was essentially the heartbeat of Babylon – and Babylon, as we referred to in the last chapter, is portrayed as the ultimate rival to God's design for human flourishing. God's decision therefore to choose a man from this city is not accidental or coincidental. It is overwhelmingly redemptive! God is choosing a man from the epicentre of an idolatrous and rebellious civilization, to begin the process of redeeming broken humanity and transforming all nations. Wow!

'So Abram went, as the LORD had told him.'[3] A simple sentence. A radical obedience. Abram has heard the echo of Eden, 'Where are you?' and rather than run from God he starts to walk with him. Noticeably Abram starts walking WEST. After all these years of people walking east, away from the presence of God, someone is now walking west! God has found a friend who will walk with him into the horizon of his own dream.

As stunning as this plan sounds, though, it is equally absurd. The promise to father a nation that would bless the whole of humanity is given to a 75-year-old nomad whose wife is barren. The promise is so absurd that Abram, despite his growing faith in God, can't really believe it's true. How can the call to reproduce blessing throughout the nations be given to an old man with a barren wife who can't reproduce anything?

A stone-cold reality is staring him square in the face. He has no son.

He will have to wait. And wait. And *wait*.

The proposal

Ten years after God called Abram to leave home, Abram hears the Voice again in a vision. The Voice speaks truth, cutting through Abram's distorted reality of who he is and who God is, untangling him from the ancient snares of fear and shame:

> Do not be afraid, Abram.
>> I am your shield,
>> your very great reward.[4]

These anchoring words to a weary and waiting heart are God's way of saying to Abram, *In your waiting I am more than enough for you, I exceed anything I ever promised you.* God is teaching Abram his presence precedes his promise.

Think of this moment as God's engagement to Abram. God is pledging his commitment to him. God cannot give Abram the fullness of the promise before he has given him himself. As broken creatures we will always find ways to short-circuit holy intimacy, but God's perfect love never will. Promise without presence misses the point!

By this stage, however, Abram's faith muscles have grown weak and disappointment has seeped into his soul. He responds in protest:

> But Abram said, 'Sovereign Lord, what can you give me since I remain childless?'[5]

To paraphrase Abram's response: *Lord, I know you've said you love me and I really want to be with you, but ultimately I don't know if you are going to come through for me.*

Abram's retort should not be dismissed simply as that of a tired and spoiled child. He is responding with genuine brokenness and disappointment. Ten long years of waiting have taken a heavy toll on him. His disappointment moves him to make a suggestion: Eliezer, a member of his household and therefore not his own son, could be the heir?

Have you ever tried to help God out? 'Here's my idea for how we could do it, God!?'

God responds with patient love and clarity: 'This man [Eliezer] will not be your heir, but a son who is your own flesh and blood will be your heir.'[6] Then God walks Abram out of his tent and invites him to lift his head. 'Look up at the sky and count the stars – if indeed you can count them . . . So shall your offspring be.'[7]

Imagine Abram's heart suddenly starting to beat again, as he sees his destiny written in the myriad of stars lighting up the night sky.

Essentially God is saying, 'Abram – look up, my boy! Even though you can't see it – even though it seems absurd and impossible – I have not forgotten you! If I can create all the stars of the sky, I can bring forth my promise to you, my son.'

The One who spoke the universe into being, calling each star by name, is expanding Abram's heart to carry what he could never have imagined carrying: stewardship of God's own dream for the world. Bewildered, Abram somehow offers up his trust to God: 'Abram believed the LORD, and he credited it to him as righteousness.'[8]

This is the biblical language of wholehearted trust and full surrender in the goodness of God when you don't know the details of what that will mean for your future. This kind of relentless trust is the basis for right-relationship (righteousness) with the Living God.

The words spoken between God and Abram in Genesis 15 are not mechanistic dialogue or superficial small-talk. This is the language of friendship, the emotive speech of love. In biblical terminology this is the language of covenant. We've mentioned the principle of covenant previously, but Abram's story is the perfect time to dive deeper.

Covenant

Covenant is very different from the modern way we define commitment. Today we talk about contracts. Contracts are formal documents written to describe a commitment between two parties, defined by a set of terms, such as the length of commitment, the level of commitment and what each party can expect in return for fulfilling their side of the contract. They ensure expectations are clear between two or more parties, and the interests of the individuals on both sides of the relationship are protected from one another.

This is not necessarily wrong; in fact it is healthy to ensure boundaries and expectations are clear when entering into serious agreements with other parties; but it is important to state emphatically, this is not how God does relationship. Further, it is not the basis upon which God wants to establish his family on the earth. God's idea of family is built upon the cornerstone of covenant. A simple definition of covenant is: 'All that I am and have is yours and all that you are and have is mine.' The main distinction between a covenant and a contract is based on the underlying principle of rights. If I sign a contract, generally speaking, I am seeking to protect and enforce my rights within that particular agreement, which means I would be stating my terms. A covenant, however, is pretty much the opposite. If I enter into a covenant, I am ultimately giving up my rights; you don't really have any of your own terms! Covenant is established on sacrificial love for the other and is marked by sacrifice, forgiveness, faithfulness and loyalty.

The symbolism of the ceremony Genesis 15 goes on to describe seals God's engagement to Abram and confirms the holy nature of covenant. God is the great initiator in this proposal. God lays a table for Abram. The animals God asks Abram to place on the table are cut in two – side by side – symbolizing the giving of oneself on behalf of the other. God is opening up his heart to Abram in this most intimate of encounters. Not unlike Adam in Eden, Abram is put into a deep sleep and a blazing torch moves between God and Abram. God speaks a hard word about slavery and affliction in the future for Abram's descendants but this word also contains a hopeful promise: one day they will return to inherit the land God has promised them.

On that day the LORD made a covenant with Abram.[9]

In these moments the aroma of the dead animals, signifying the death of oneself for the other, is transformed into the sweetest fragrance of sacrificial love. Abram's heart is fused with the divine in perfect oneness. Joined with God, through a symbolic ritual of death, Abram ironically has never been more alive. The depth of loving union God invites Abram into has melted his heart, allowing it to become a warm and receptive seedbed, where the seed of promise could thrive. In doing so, God has irrevocably bound himself to Abram. This is what covenant is all about.

Abram's mistake

Even after this beautiful and profound engagement ceremony, The God Story reminds us how deeply flawed Abram is. Conspiring with his wife Sarai, Abram figures God needs his help to see the promise fulfilled. His method is a complete abuse of power and privilege. Abram sleeps with Hagar, Sarai's maidservant, and Hagar is forced to conceive. Nine months later a son called Ishmael is born. In pushing things forward at his own pace, Abram has to deal with the devastating consequences of this selfish decision. A lesson many of us have had to learn through life when we take a word from God and try to fulfil it in our own way. The result is usually damage for us and, as we see in Abram's case, even more damage to others.

And yet, as we see with Abram, God will not give up on us. Moreover, he will work redemptively through our mistakes. God has made a covenant with Abram and is in it for the long haul. God will not let him settle for less than what he promised. Abram will have to learn. He is still not ready to receive the magnitude of blessing God wants to release on him and through him.

God's encounter with Hagar also deserves to be told. In the Genesis account of Abram and Sarai's story some may presume the fearful and despised Hagar will simply play an 'outlier' role. Surely it would be more convenient for everyone if this shamed pregnant slave girl just slipped out of the story quickly and quietly, her role remembered as a small blip in the storyline?

But The God Story ensures Hagar's story will be told, as will the stories of many other so-called 'outliers' as the biblical narrative unfolds.[10] Nobody just 'makes up the numbers' in The God Story. Everyone matters, for everything counts, before the One who will redeem all. More, God will not allow Hagar's story to simply serve as an uncomfortable reminder of Abram's sin. Rather, Hagar will be remembered as a courageous woman who risked her life and that of her precious son to leave her master's house, refusing to remain in a place of abuse and oppression. Hagar is the woman God will not leave to be used and then discarded shamefully. In fact it is this story – God's pursuit of an abused slave girl into the desert – which unveils one of his most personal names for the very first time. Hagar, astounded by God's merciful revelation to her and his promise of commitment to her and her son, in the presence of Love, experiences the fear and shame she once felt dissolve inside of her. She can only exclaim, '*El Roi*', 'the God who sees me'.[11]

The marriage

It's hard not to wonder if Abram found himself looking at his son Ishmael throughout these years, hoping that the promised seed of blessing would be multiplied through his firstborn child. Surely God could simply sidestep Abram's previous mistake and shoehorn the universal plan of redemption through Ishmael? After all, there was no other option now – not at his age. If not through Eliezer or Ishmael, then who?

But as we come to Genesis 17, almost 25 years after the original promise was given and 14 years after Ishmael was born, it appears Abram has matured in trust. We can only conclude God has used these years to tenderly carve Abram's heart into a holy receptacle now ready to carry God's dream for the world.

The waiting is about to come to an end.

If Genesis 15 tells us of God's engagement to Abram, then Genesis 17, 14 years later, records the marriage. The core elements of what we would expect in a traditional marriage are laid out in the text. First of all, God appears to Abram in glorious splendour, revealing through his name the terms of the covenant:

> I am God Almighty; walk before me, and be blameless, that I may make my covenant between me and you, and may multiply you greatly.[12]

This is the first time God describes himself as 'God Almighty'. *El Shaddai* in Hebrew speaks of God's power, protection and provision and sets a new pattern. God will refer to who he is in this way when the covenant is reaffirmed in generations to come. Abram, undone by God's glorious invitation, responds in mutual loving surrender: 'Abram fell facedown.'[13] Second, the covenant is symbolized by circumcision, not unlike the giving of rings in marriage or a permanent tattoo of your partner's name on your body. Third, a reformulation of identity takes place as a new name is conferred upon Abram, just like a bride will bear the name of her spouse in many cultures around the world today. Abram becomes Abraham. Sarai, who has endured her own disappointment and long wait, is also acknowledged by God. Validated for her resilient faith, Sarai's name is changed to Sarah. Abram and Sarai's journey into true identity has reached a maturation point. Abraham and Sarah have now become the father and mother of nations. The word 'become' here is important. It speaks to the process of spiritual formation. Abram became what he was destined to inherit. Or as Eugene Peterson translates it, 'Abraham was first named "father" and then *became* a father because he dared to trust God to do what only God could do.'[14] This is a central theme of The God Story. We become people of promise before we inherit the promise. Identity precedes destiny. And continual trust is needed every step of the way in the 'becoming'.

Now the covenant is made, the waiting is almost over and the fruit of their faith will birth the promise. God declares that by the same time next year they will have a child.[15]

Isaac will be born at the perfect time – when the full work of relinquishment is complete and wholehearted trust is all that defines God's relationship with Abraham. Ishmael came through control and human manufacturing; the son of promise could only come through wonder, joy and loving surrender. Abraham only happens to be 100 and Sarah 90! They name their boy Isaac because it means laughter! The whole process has been so absurd and humanly impossible – Abraham's body as good as dead and Sarah's womb completely barren – they can do nothing but laugh. 'Is anything too hard for the LORD?'[16] The incredulous laughter of unbelief has been transformed into joy-filled belly-laughs of promise-fulfilment.

The ultimate test of trust

In the remaining days of Abraham's life The God Story reveals a man of *presence* – a friend of God who has grown old in holy and intimate union with his covenant partner. God can hear the echo of his own heart in the prayers and intercessions of Abraham.[17] He has become the quintessential picture of a friend of God despite his many failures.

One might think Abraham's story should end here. But it doesn't. Abraham is faced with his greatest test of all. The climactic event recorded in Abraham's life takes place on a mountain called Moriah. We turn to Genesis 22 to read one of the most famous and challenging passages of Scripture in the Judeo-Christian tradition:

> Some time later God tested Abraham. He said to him, 'Abraham!'
>
> 'Here I am,' he replied.
>
> Then God said, 'Take your son, your only son, whom you love – Isaac – and go to the region of Moriah. Sacrifice him there as a burnt offering on a mountain I will show you.'[18]

There is a danger that those of us overfamiliar with this story may miss the layers of human emotion triggered through a fresh reading of this event. God's request to Abraham is supposed to cause a visceral reaction within us. God asks Abraham to do the unthinkable! First of all, on the surface it doesn't make sense: after all these years of waiting for a son to be born who would carry the promise, now, before Isaac has had children of his own, God wants Abraham to give him up? Seriously, God? Second, there is a part of us tempted to reject a God who asks any father to sacrifice his son.

And yet we read on. The narrative of Genesis 22 pulls us into the holy mystery of an event that dramatically foreshadows the climax of The God Story many years later.

We can only imagine what Abraham is experiencing in his heart as he walks with Isaac up the side of Mount Moriah. Isaac, who is unaware of God's instructions to his father, innocently assumes they are going up a mountain for a time of worship together. Naturally he enquires, 'Father . . . where is the lamb?'[19] Abraham responds, 'God himself will provide the lamb.'[20] A prophetic phrase, the ultimate definition of God's provision of sacrificial love,[21] that will echo down through history.

But does Abraham really know the meaning of what he is saying? Is Abraham simply deceiving his son? Or what if Abraham has reached that place of wholehearted trust in God where deep down in his soul he knows God will come through?

Most likely, these are moments of unthinkable emotional trauma for Abraham. Imagine tears running down Abraham's face as his trembling hand lifts the knife. Listen for his desperate groans as he cries out for another way. Picture the terrified look on the innocent face of his teenage son bound to the wood, laid on the altar. Abraham is experiencing the unrelenting tension of 'God as Tester' and 'God as Provider' simultaneously.[22] He knows God is testing him, he knows the Great Lover of his soul is asking him to own up to his sins and failures, completely renounce any self-entitled scheming and surrender the future of his family to God.[23] Yet after all these years of walking with God, Abraham has also grown in confidence in God's nature and provision. That Abraham eventually lifts the knife above his son shows his willingness to trust in God's provision no matter the cost.

Then, in these aw(e)ful moments of terror, hear the Voice of divine provision break in:

But the angel of the LORD called out to him from heaven, 'Abraham, Abraham!'

'Here I am,' he replied.

'Do not lay a hand on the boy,' he said. 'Do not do anything to him. Now I know that you fear God, because you have not withheld from me your son, your only son.'[24]

Imagine Abraham collapsing in relief as he embraces his precious and promised son, holding him more tightly than he ever has before. And Isaac, partly confused, partly traumatized yet now wholly comforted in the embrace of his father – more loved than he has ever been. Imagine his bewildered cry, 'Dad, who is this God?' as this teenage boy seeks to wrap his head around the intense jealousy of the God of his father. And yet in a world where child sacrifice to the gods was not uncommon, ponder the wonderful realization dawning upon Isaac: his life has been spared, God has provided another sacrifice and a great calling rests upon his life. This is *Jehovah Jireh* – God our Provider. Isaac's soul has been indelibly marked by this display of sacrificial love and the faith it inspires will mean Isaac will carry the essence of The God Story to the next generations.

Finally, imagine the holy pause in the throne room of heaven. Feel the weight of God's words to Abraham, 'Now I know.' Abraham has completely won the heart of God. His obedience in this most sacred of moments reveals that our choice to completely surrender can move God's heart in breathtaking wonder.

God can be completely satisfied that the seed of promise is blossoming in the heart of his closest companion on the earth. Isaac may have been the sacrifice laid on the altar, but God really wanted Abraham. It's no wonder this is where we find the first mention of worship in the Bible. Worship and sacrifice are inseparable. Abraham, who received this promise many years ago and has not always fully believed, is now presented to us as a son who totally embodies the essence of The God Story – only those who die to themselves know how to truly live; only those who give up the gift can truly receive the Giver; only those who lay down the promise can receive the fullness of his presence.

The seed multiplies

Abraham dies a few years later, but before he does he asks his servant to find a bride for Isaac. Isaac takes Rebekah to be his wife, but like his parents they struggle to have children. Isaac, carrying the story of his own miraculous conception, trusts in the word of the Lord and contends for the same promise. He waits 20 years for his prayers to be answered. It appears God has all the time in the world, if it means transforming his broken image-bearers into sons and daughters prepared to partner with him for the flourishing of creation.

Once again, the plot moves miraculously forward through a barren womb. Twins are born, Jacob and Esau, who will help define the phrase 'sibling rivalry'. Esau, the older by a few minutes, sells his birthright for something cheap: a bowl of soup. Jacob initially appears to us as a conniving fraud and trickster. Having acquired the rights of the firstborn, Jacob goes one step further. Taking advantage of Isaac's aging eyesight, he disguises himself before his dad as his brother Esau and steals the blessing normally reserved for the firstborn. In doing so Jacob steps into the flow of blessing from his grandfather (Abraham) and his father (Isaac). Despite his deeply flawed character Jacob becomes the living channel through which God's promise is passed. But he has to escape to live in this blessing because Esau wants revenge. Jacob's safe place is Harran and in particular his uncle Laban's farm. On his way there he stops for a night's sleep. During the night Jacob dreams of a ladder stretching between heaven and earth upon which angels ascend and descend. The dream is a vivid picture of God's great desire for the world: the overlapping and interlocking of heaven and earth. If Jacob is going to carry the seed of promise, God knows he needs his own encounter. In the dream God declares, 'I am the LORD, the God of your father Abraham and the God of Isaac. I will give you and your descendants the land on which you are lying.'[25]

Not unlike his grandfather, Jacob's stewardship of God's dream involves an intense process of development. With great blessing comes great responsibility. God may not have stopped him from stealing the blessing but he would not let him think it came cheap. Jacob needs serious work. He needs to be chiselled, shaped and formed into a suitable partner for God. To be chosen by God means to be moulded into a vessel fit to overflow with love of the Eternal Family, so others can be drawn into the purposes of God. Jacob has to submit to the process.

After 20 years of straightening out, Jacob finally meets with God again. God comes to Jacob in the dark of night and they begin to wrestle together. Jacob intuitively realizes that this is a necessary fight. He knows the One he is holding in his arms possesses everything he needs to be truly satisfied, and so he will not let him go. Jacob wrestles with God all night. 'I will not let you go unless you bless me,'[26] Jacob cries out when God tries to leave. Only a divine submission, a holy force of loving power, could break Jacob's resistance. Jacob is wounded and walks with a limp from that point on, but that short-term jab of wincing pain is a price Jacob is willing to pay if it results in long-term wholeness.

Jacob names the place he wrestled with God 'Peniel', meaning literally 'face of God'. Jacob helps us realize the place of our deepest wounding can become our moment of greatest healing, for even here in the darkest night the radiance of God's face shines upon us. Jacob's identity is deepened at Peniel, his true personhood further formed and his original destiny realized. God is pleased to declare over him, 'Your name will no longer be Jacob, but Israel.'[27]

Jacob has come full circle. He eventually reunites with Esau and gives him back a blessing. But in God's eternal purposes the seed of promise will still pass through Jacob. His 12 sons – Reuben, Simeon, Levi, Judah, Dan, Naphtali, Gad, Asher, Issachar, Zebulun, Joseph and Benjamin – will form the heads of the 12 tribes of Israel in the formation of a nation we will discuss in the next chapter.

Jacob's penultimate son, Joseph, deserves a brief mention considering a sizable amount of the book of Genesis is devoted to his life story. We are introduced to him as a prodigious young man possessing dazzling prophetic revelation but equal measures of pride. Discarded by his brothers we follow his life from a pit to a palace – Potiphar's house – where he overcomes temptations and endures the injustice of false accusations, the results of which land him in prison. Eventually vindicated by God, he is raised up to a position of extraordinary influence in the great empire of Egypt, second in power only to Pharaoh. Great favour rests on his life, and the supernatural wisdom he is endowed with enables him to steward God's blessing to the nations. In a divinely orchestrated twist, Joseph's own brothers, who tragically disowned him and presumed him dead, find their way to Egypt to beg for Joseph's help in a time of famine.

In a stunning show of grace, Joseph confers mercy and forgiveness on his undeserving brothers and is reconciled with his family. In the end he is able to declare, 'You meant evil against me, but God meant it for good.'[28] What started as a tragic rejection for Joseph, God redeemed into a miraculous salvation for his people.

This statement in the final words of Genesis is a beautiful way to summarize God's gracious and redemptive hand in the dramatic story of Joseph's life. But more broadly, it is a succinct articulation of the story to date. 'What you meant for evil, God meant for good' gets to the heart of the dynamic blessings contained within the seed of promise that was planted in Joseph's great-grandfather, Abraham, more than 100 years previously.

In fact, if we draw a line from Eden in Genesis 1 to the end of Joseph's story in the final chapter of Genesis, we can conclude: despite the fragility of the plot, owing to humankind's own attempts to literally write their own self-centred script and the ongoing influence of the devil, the story has been preserved and redemption is under way.

Divine blessing has multiplied through the sons of Abraham's line. Despite their obvious sins he, Isaac and Jacob have said YES to God, and now through their sons and daughters a hopeful seed of promise has found its way into the dark womb of Egypt.

A small and insignificant nomadic tribe with a host of dysfunctional issues have been caught up in the eternal purposes of God for the world.

Presence: God gave Abraham a spectacular promise: blessing to all nations. But God had to teach Abraham the ultimate promise was his presence! God alone was Abraham's reward! The seed of God's promise could only be planted in a heart totally surrendered to and in perfect friendship with God. As Abraham laid Isaac on the altar, God knew he had found the right person to carry his dream for the world.

Family: God's way to win all the families of the earth was through a family. Through Abraham's faith, passed on to his many sons and daughters, the promise of blessing to all would come. Covenant was how God would seal his intimate relationship with Abraham and his descendants – a promise to give everything you are and will be for the sake of the other. Covenant was the cornerstone of the family God wanted to form on the earth, a reflection of the love of the Eternal Family.

Kingdom: God's desire to fill the earth with his loving rule and reign is contained in his radical promise to Abraham – through you all nations will be blessed – which will pass through Abraham to all of humankind. The original dream of Eden extending through the earth is back on track. Abraham's story teaches us God's kingdom will not come through human striving and engineering (Ishmael) but through joyful surrender and trust (Isaac). When God finds this kind of faith and trust, the supernatural power of his kingdom will be released, even in bodies as good as dead.

Father, help us, like Abraham and Sarah, to hear your voice wooing us away from the familiar, to come and walk with you. Help us to trust in your promise over our lives even though we can't see how it will unfold. Forgive us when we try to engineer your plans in our own strength. Help us to wholeheartedly surrender to you so we can play our part.

Questions for reflection: Where are you being invited to trust God and follow his voice no matter the cost? Is there any area in your life where you are trying to engineer God's promise in your own wisdom instead of wholeheartedly trusting God's plan?

4

The Birth of a Nation

The opening scenes of Exodus do not paint a pretty picture. The favour Jacob's family had enjoyed under Joseph's exceptional leadership eventually ended, dissolving into a devastating regime of slavery under the tyrannical rule of another Egyptian Pharoah 'who did not know Joseph'.[1] And yet, beneath it all, the seed of promise is still growing. The Eden-call to 'be fruitful and multiply' has followed the descendants of Abraham into Egypt. In fact, estimates reckon Israel has multiplied from a meagre extended family of 70 people to a tribal movement of 2 million! Even though these hard days were foretold in God's promise to Abraham[2] 400 years earlier, God is still with them.

The dark empire of Egypt

The Pharaoh of the day is obsessed with power. Like all narcissistic leaders, underneath his public power plays he is insecure and driven by fear at the thought of losing control. Concerned by the Israelites' birth control mechanisms (or lack of them!) and the threat posed to his powerbase, Pharoah introduces three particular forms of oppression. The first is his harsh regime of slavery, which involves the Israelites making bricks for the Egyptian Empire. Second, he commands the Hebrew[3] midwives to kill the Hebrew babies when they are delivering them (these courageous heroines refuse to be dominated by the system!). Lastly, in delusionary frenzy, Pharoah decides to abort a generation, commanding all the baby boys to be thrown into a river and drowned.

Throughout the Exodus narrative, Egypt under Pharoah's leadership provides a vivid example of the empire pattern we have established in 'The Fall' when describing the City and Tower of

Babel. Empires are rich 'superpowers' believing they have a divine right to rule and shape history according to their will. To achieve this they employ a politics of oppression, flexing their muscles economically and geopolitically, backed up by the lurking threat their military provides. They are bullies. The 'gods' of these empires reside over the social order, reinforcing the status of the elite and manipulating systems of enterprise to serve themselves. It always results in the exploitation of the poor.

The Exodus narrative wants to make it explicitly clear that the force of God's kingdom is set against these empires. Egypt is the polar opposite to God's vision for freedom; empire consciousness, where humans are reduced to utilities and nameless tools, is the antithesis of the loving reign of God. The story of Israel's deliverance will bear witness to a subversive holy plan, initiated from heaven, for no less than the complete dismantling of the Egyptian Empire. Judgement Day is coming.

God has heard the cries and groans of the oppressed.

He still does.

Moses

For the children of Israel the stark reality Exodus presents to Abraham's descendants is that they are *not* living in any of the original promises that God gave him: (1) they are not a nation, (2) they don't have a land and (3) they find themselves bound in slavery rather than living in blessing. All they have are whispers of a distant story.

Four hundred years later Abraham's children look nothing like a defined constituted nation but resemble a sprawling large and diverse mixture of refugees. In pure historical terms, it is a marvel they survived. By all accounts, humanly speaking, the children of Israel should have been snuffed out, sucked into the vortex of history like other tribal people groups that would have been captured by powerful empires like Egypt.

The channel of deliverance for this bunch of slaves comes through a man destined to become their leader since he was a baby boy. Moses' life story is so riveting, scary and exhilarating that it deserves a book of its own. As a baby Moses was hidden among the reeds of the river by his mother during Pharaoh's genocide of the Hebrew babies. He was found by Pharaoh's daughter as she went to bathe. Her heart was tenderized by the vulnerable state of this baby boy and she took him home to the palace. Pharaoh's daughter unwittingly assigns Moses' mother to come to the royal court to help wean him. Imagine the favour and providential grace of God here as he inconspicuously weaves his sovereign plan through tragedy, oppression and persecution. This is no fairy tale. The pain, grief and trial experienced by God's people in the power-hungry vortex of the Egyptian Empire are the context through which God's redemptive thread is being woven.

One can only imagine the paradoxical nature of Moses' development – enjoying the privileges and pomp of the Egyptian Empire but at the same time being told the story of his own oppressed people and their God by his faithful mother. As the boy Moses grew to become a man, the internal conflict of both these influences eventually became too much for him. This acute dissonance he felt inside boiled over one day when he saw an Egyptian cruelly beating an Israelite. In this moment, Moses' years of battling false identity exploded in uncontrollable rage. He retaliated, beating the Egyptian soldier to death. Moses' reaction speaks powerfully to the truth that any movement of justice fuelled by human anger and tainted by bitterness rather than tempered by brokenness and formed in unconditional love will not bring about the justice of God.

Flooded with regret and more unsure than he'd ever been of where he belonged, Moses had to get away. He fled to the desert. He then wandered around the backside of the Sinai peninsula for 40 years, working for his father-in-law in Midian as a lowly shepherd. The 'Prince of Egypt' endured a severe humbling, living out what appeared to be an unfulfilled second half of life. Forty years of life in the palace with all its privileges had become a distant memory. He was at the end of himself. Moses thought he would never come out of Midian again. But God is just getting started with him.

The story isn't over.

The burning bush

One day Moses, now 80, while following his sheep around the desert, notices a burning bush. The intrigue around *this* particular bush for Moses on this particular day is that the bush burning is not being destroyed or consumed. It stops Moses in his tracks: 'I will go over and see this strange sight – why the bush does not burn up.'[4]

As Moses turns aside, God speaks his name. 'Moses! Moses!'[5] No one can say our name like God. Imagine, after all these years, Moses is hearing his own personal name, spoken not by the imperial court but by the living God.

Moses is one of a number[6] of image-bearers we will meet in The God Story who respond with the same radical availability: 'Here I am!'[7] Moses' response means anything can happen now. God has found another partner. This is holy ground.

Moses must take off his shoes.

Through the symbolism of the bush, crackling with fire yet not consumed, God is communicating something deep to Moses. He wants Moses to know something new is happening to him: God's love is going to burn up every false and unformed part of him, in order that he might become who he was created to be.

Can you see what is happening here? Moses is being invited to play a central role in the unfolding story. To confirm this, God welcomes him into the redemptive flow of blessing given to his forefathers: 'I am the God of your father, the God of Abraham, the God of Isaac and the God of Jacob.'[8]

Then God begins to reveal his heart to Moses:

The LORD said, 'I have indeed seen the misery of my people in Egypt. I have heard them crying out because of their slave drivers, and I am concerned about their suffering. So I have come down to rescue them from the hand of the Egyptians and to bring them up out of that land into a good and spacious land.'[9]

Moses' encounter is unfolding more of the beauty of God's heart and character. God has not forgotten Abraham's descendants. He unashamedly declares the Hebrew slaves 'my people'. He has *seen* their misery. He has *heard* their crying. He has been *moved* by their suffering. He will *come down* to deliver them. God is identifying with the least, the slave, those at the bottom of the social ladder. Further, he promises not a socially distanced response but an intimate and involved one. He will 'come down' and rescue them. The God of the universe is emphatically stating he is a co-suffering partner to the vulnerable and oppressed, the used and abused.

How will God rescue them?

So now, go. I am sending you to Pharaoh to bring my people the Israelites out of Egypt.[10]

The way God will rescue the Hebrew slaves is through the leadership of Moses. Moses will be God's mediator. He will speak the word of God in the heart of darkness.

Moses' response to such a commission is a mixture of shock, confusion and deep insecurity. *Who? Me? What?* First of all, he can't understand the logic in being told to go back to Pharaoh, who most likely wants him dead, with the instruction that he needs to change his regime simply because some 'foreign' God said so! Can anyone identify with Moses here? Second, his words ('Who am I that I should go to Pharaoh?'[11]) reveal a distorted and diminished identity. God responds with the assurance of his presence ('I will be with you'[12]) and the promise of a sign ('you will worship God on this mountain'[13]). Moses pushes back to God with a legitimate question: 'Suppose I go to the Israelites and say to them, "The God of your fathers has sent me to you," and they ask me, "What is his name?" Then what shall I tell them?'[14]

Through this question Moses has opened the door for God to reveal his eternal and most personal Name, at this point of The God Story. We have come to one of the most sacred moments in Scripture.

This is holy ground. Maybe we should take off our shoes too.

YHWH – infinite and intimate

God said to Moses, 'I AM WHO I AM. This is what you are to say to the Israelites: "I AM has sent me to you."'[15]

'I am who I am'. In Hebrew The Name is simply four letters – YHWH. Theologians call this the tetragrammaton, which literally means 'four letters', and it is from these we derive the name *Yahweh*. Jewish Rabbis, on the other hand, simply refer to it as 'The Name'. For them, the pure, personal presence of God is so ineffable and holy they will not repeat it.

Over the years, various suggestions have been made concerning the actual meaning of YHWH. Scholarly consensus has landed on something close to, 'I am who I am', or, 'I will be who I will be.' God is essentially saying to Moses, 'You cannot comprehend me fully, you can't box me, I am beyond your terms and categories description!' Moses is being reminded that the God of his forefathers is the ultimate wellspring of all being, the Holy Originator of life, who has absolute confidence and humble security in his own identity. This undefinable nature of 'I am who I am' is the only appropriate name for the incomparable God of the universe. Yet in these moments Yahweh has come close to Moses to say he is intimately acquainted with the pain of his people. From this point on we must carry forward a holy tension when we think about God. Yahweh is both infinite and intimate, transcendent and immanent, majestic and approachable, undefinable yet knowable. As C. S. Lewis puts it, 'God is both further from us, and nearer to us, than any other being.'[16]

God sealed this revelation to Moses with the immortal words:

This is my name for ever,
  the name you shall call me
  from generation to generation.[17]

Vulnerable and fragile, stubborn and hard

Despite the profundity and sacredness of Moses' encounter with God, Moses is still unconvinced. His complex past has shattered his confidence. He is bound up by fear and shame. At this point Moses is the quintessential 'reluctant leader'. It becomes apparent that Moses, emptied of his own self-confidence, is in the perfect place to become a true partner of God. To prove it, God asks Moses to lay down his rod. A rod was a natural symbol of authority in ancient culture and in laying it down Moses is divesting himself of his own (false) identity, his source of income and any influence he has left in life. God then invites him to pick the rod back up again. Moses is now ready to step into his original design and his God-given identity for the first time in his life. He will become one of the greatest leaders who ever lived. The process has been crucial, though; the wilderness has done its work. Authority in the hands of a leader not broken by his own sense of fragility is dangerous. Now marked by brokenness, suffering and humility, Moses at this point in life has never carried more authority. Moses is ready.

With his elder brother Aaron at his side, Moses proceeds to Pharaoh delivering the news: 'God says, "Let my people go so they may worship me."' Pharaoh laughs their request out of his royal court and then increases the workload on the Hebrew slaves. This of course doesn't get Moses' leadership reputation off to a great start.

God is not perturbed. Pharaoh and the princes of Egypt are going to find out the hard way how valuable the Hebrew lives are to God. It will take some convincing – a series of plagues are dealt out – water turning to blood, frogs, lice, flies, livestock pestilence, boils, hail, locusts, darkness. These plagues are not random displays of God's power. This is the intentional and systematic dismantling of Egypt's local deities, and with each plague comes an opportunity for Pharaoh to repent. Pharaoh hardens his heart each time. He thinks he can match the 'magic' of this Hebrew God, but after the third plague, his gods are exposed and have no answer.

Passover

The last plague carries the most devastating effect for Pharaoh and his regime. An angel of death will pass over the nation. Unless Pharoah releases the Hebrew slaves a devastating blow will come to Egypt: the firstborn son of every home will die. Pharaoh refuses again to let the Israelites go, and a great cry is heard in Egypt that night. The Israelites, however, are spared. God, through Moses, has instructed the Israelites to take a male spotless lamb, sacrifice it and place blood on the doorposts of their homes as they partake in their last meal in Egypt together. The sign of a lamb's blood would deliver them from the angel of death and from this night on would become symbolic of their liberation from slavery. This event is of course the birth of the still-practised Passover Feast, the principal commemoration of the children of Israel's deliverance from slavery and the meal that will shape their consciousness for many generations to come.

Red Sea

Pharaoh's stubbornness has been broken. He allows the Israelites to go, after 400 years of slavery. For now at least. A vast caravan of Hebrew slaves is about to start walking out of Egypt. Imagine them beginning to consider a new life of freedom after hundreds of years of bondage. They aren't quite sure where they are going but they know they have a chance to leave their past, and that is good enough. There are no signs of any social infrastructure to their community yet: no laws, no sanitation, no leadership structure. To guide them, a fire by night and a cloud by day – symbols of the presence of God. The directions are simply, 'follow the cloud'; 'go with the fire'; 'move with the presence'. It will take the Hebrew slaves some time to learn how to rely on the presence of YHWH, starting with the prospect of a wall of voracious water staring them in the face. The seeming impossibility of venturing through the Red Sea is made more intimidating by the fact that Pharaoh, realizing that he has lost his free slave labour, changes his mind and decides to deploy his whole army to pursue and recapture the Israelites. Imagine the Israelites flooded by fear of the vast impasse in front of them, the angry Egyptian army behind. What on earth do they do?!

Moses may be still a work-in-progress but he has begun to realize there is something about this God that can be trusted even in the most extreme situations. He has matured from a quivering, insecure man to a calm and assured leader, able to listen above the noise of the circumstances around him to another Voice. He replies to the people:

> Do not be afraid. Stand firm and you will see the deliverance the LORD will bring you today. The Egyptians you see today you will never see again. The LORD will fight for you; you need only to be still.[18]

Moses stretches his hand over the Red Sea and as he does a wind moves upon the waters, pulling them back so there is dry ground for the Israelites to walk on. We are told there is darkness for the Egyptians while the Israelites walk through in the light! As they do, an act of new creation is happening. Water and land are separated again, darkness and light are once again distinguished, as the God who once moved over the watery chaos is doing it again. Nothing less than a re-enactment of creation is taking place through God's sovereign power and grace. This is no local deity; the God who created the heavens and the earth is now forming a people, a new nation, unto himself.

Ponder the Hebrew slaves walking between two walls of water. As they reach the other side, they watch the Egyptians follow them headlong into the dry land between the waters. Confusion besets the Egyptians and their chariots begin to break up. Moses stretches out his hand over the sea once again. As he does, the walls of water close in upon the Egyptians and they are completely submerged. Imagine the noise as roaring waves crash down forcefully on everything that represents their past, hundreds of years of oppression and slavery swallowed in the sea.

Picture the shock sweeping through the vast crowd of startled refugees now standing on the other side of the Red Sea. As tears of joyful relief stream down their faces, imagine the sound of a mighty shout of triumph erupting as 2 million voices – men, women, boys and girls – burst forth in ecstatic rapture, for all their enemies have been defeated: 'The LORD is my strength and my song, and he has become my salvation.'[19]

The Exodus narrative, the archetypal freedom story, never grows old. It's no wonder this story has been rehearsed throughout Israel's history. It has inspired many movements of liberation, but first and foremost this is a salvation story – God doing for humankind what we can't do for ourselves. Freedom is our destiny; salvation is our story. The Exodus of Israel is pregnant with foreshadowing of the liberation of the whole cosmos. An even greater light will shine in the pages to come and a path will be cleared for all of humanity to be saved and walk into freedom.

The gift of the wilderness

As the wild celebrations begin to settle and the Hebrews gaze into a barren wilderness, you can picture them asking each other the question: what are we going to do now? A new beginning has dawned, but what are God's intentions for the Israelites now that they are free? God's original promise to their forefather Abraham reminds us of the answer. God has a glorious inheritance for them. They may still think of themselves as slaves but they are destined to be a blessed people overflowing with blessing to the nations. And God promised to provide them a land.[20] But to live in a promised land will mean learning how to become a promise people.

To do this they will need to go through the wilderness. It will not be easy, but residual patterns of slavery will have to go if they are one day going to inherit a land. God has taken them out of Egypt, but he will need to take 'Egypt' out of them. The complexities of transitioning from authoritarian rule in Egypt to becoming the loving family of God begin to manifest themselves almost straight away. 'Oh, for the meat of Egypt,' they cry just days later, craving the food of slavery rather than trusting the provision of a rescuing God.[21] This type of exposure is the work of the wilderness, a painful gift, revealing our attachments and weaning us off our false distorted identities. After years of slavery, the everyday meagre goal of survival has conditioned in them a 'poverty spirit', fear and shame driving everything. Yet the God who is perfect love commits to the process of driving out fear. Like a loving father, God provides them with their basic human need. Food! Manna (meaning, 'what is it?') is the bread God miraculously gives to his people each day. Daily bread is provided to teach daily reliance on God as the source of their very life. Wilderness is not a place of punishment but the place where holy patterns are scribed on our hearts, preparing us for the inheritance ahead.

A royal identity

The sheer audaciousness of God's plan for the former slaves comes into full view in Exodus 19. At this point Moses has instructed the people to set up camp at the bottom of a mountain called Sinai, and it is here God speaks.

> The LORD called to him from the mountain and said, 'This is what you are to say to the descendants of Jacob and what you are to tell the people of Israel: "You yourselves have seen what I did to Egypt, and how I carried you on eagles' wings and brought you to myself. Now if you obey me fully and keep my covenant, then out of all nations you will be my treasured possession. Although the whole earth is mine, you will be for me a kingdom of priests and a holy nation."'[22]

God could not be making Israel's mission statement any clearer. He has chosen the children of Israel to be a nation who show-case his original purposes for humanity to the world. A radical new dimension of God's original promise to Abraham is being revealed to the Israelites in this encounter; an intensification in their understanding of who they are as God's covenant people. God outlines three vital and distinct elements of Israel's identity and vocation.

'You will be *my treasured possession*.' Feel the holy jealousy of these words. God wants these Hebrew slaves as his own. The whole earth still belongs to God but divine desire has chosen a specific people to cherish and set his love upon. There is nothing desirable or great, in human terms, about Israel, but God has quite simply fallen in love with these people. What must it have been like for a people who had only ever been used and abused to now be so valued, esteemed and prized?

A holy nation. 'Holy': one word to describe the incomparable beauty and multifaceted brilliance of God. Chosen by the One who is set apart in glory from all others, Israel is being constituted as distinct from other nations, to reflect the nature of God.

A kingdom of priests. In the ancient world priests stood before the gods on behalf of the people. God wanted Israel to be *his version of a priest*, connecting the beauty of God's heart with the brokenness of humanity; nothing less than a reflection of Adam's original mandate in Eden, a co-partner, extending his loving rule and reign throughout the earth.

After these three explicit affirmations of Israel's identity and vocation, God lights up the sky, a divine firework display to celebrate this union with his treasured ones.

Ten living words

As Mount Sinai continues to shake, God begins to speak ten living words. The focus now is how the Israelites are to live with and for God within his covenantal love, communicated in clear practical words, commonly known as 'The Ten Commandments'. These prohibitions are more than simple *don't-dos*. These words are *Torah*, literally, 'to guide'; Torah is God's best for us in all of life. Or, as Rabbi Jonathan Sachs says, 'love needs law and law needs love.'[23] These ten living words carry a mixture of 'vertical' (with God) and 'horizontal' (with one another) implications for their relationships. The children of Israel are to give their wholehearted allegiance to God, placing no other gods before him. Then, their love for this jealous God should be reflected in a compassionate and just community (do not murder, do not commit adultery, do not steal, do not bear false witness, do not covet). Philip Greenslade describes the Ten Commandments as 'the radical means by which the Creator God's ordering of chaos at creation is replicated at the social level, so that heaven's will is done on earth'.[24]

With the terms of the relationship made clear, Moses seals the covenant by splashing blood against the rocks and the people declare vows to the Lord: 'We will do everything the LORD has said; we will obey'.[25] A cloud covers the mountain for six days as God enfolds his treasured possession in a canopy of love. To consummate the covenant God invites Moses into the cloud. From the foothills of the mountain the people can see a fire burning in the cloud, a symbol of God's jealous love and glory.

Moses remains with God on the mountain for 40 days.

Leviticus come to life

Israel has been now constituted as a nation governed by God's basic conditions needed for healthy community living. These commandments will conflate into hundreds of other practical laws which are recorded in Exodus and make up much of the book of Leviticus. Leviticus may be difficult to read through the lens of our modern sensibilities, but within the unfolding story it makes sense.

First of all, at this stage Israel has no basic framework for a thriving society and God is kindly helping them out. What would you do with 2 million refugees in a wilderness?! Second, the Promised Land, Israel's destination, is steeped in pagan culture, reflected in a range of vile customs including promiscuous sex and child sacrifice. God wants to ensure the Israelites won't imbibe this culture as their own. They are called to be a holy nation. These laws are God's way of immersing them in his culture, fathering them in his holy ways and codifying them as a promise people. Leviticus teaches us that to worship God is to participate in a just and caring society in all of life. The standout verse right at the centre of Leviticus, 'Love your neighbour as yourself,'[26] confirms there is no holiness without social holiness. Relationship is the context for holiness. God is personal but he is never private.

Dwelling together

Before Moses is allowed back down the mountain, God reveals to him the plan for living together. The terms of covenant are not introduced to serve a distant relationship between a Master and his subjects but to allow Israel to enjoy friendship with God. The whole Exodus narrative has been building towards this moment: 'Have them make a sanctuary for me, and I will dwell among them.'[27] God wants to 'dwell' (literally 'tabernacle') in the midst of them. He longs *to be with them*. Can you feel God's eternal desire for communion with humanity expressed in these words?

So, God gives Moses a divine blueprint. A massive tent, called the tabernacle, will be the place of his habitation and presence on the earth. The tabernacle is placed in the middle of the Israelites' encampment so the people might understand that the presence of God is central to their existence. This carefully constructed marquee-type expanse will train the Israelites in a way of worship in all of life. Everything about the tabernacle is symbolic: the furniture, the designs, the colours, the way the priests are to go about their duty. All this imagery carries strong echoes of Eden, the original 'temple' where God and humanity dwelt together.

The tabernacle is therefore designed as a microcosm of the whole earth! It is constructed in three parts: 'the outer courts', 'the holy place' and 'the holy of holies', symbolizing the cosmic dream of God to fill the world with his goodness and glory. The sealed-off section called the 'holy of holies' will be the location for the Ark of the Covenant. This Ark is a huge chest-like box and is to be understood as the hot-spot of God's tangible presence on the earth. If the Israelites follow the divine pattern of worship, God promises his glory will come, and his great hope is that Israel will learn how to steward his presence beyond the holy of holies into the outer-courts (the rest of the world).

If one searches carefully through the intricate details of the tabernacle design, you will find lots of reference to ringlets and poles. Random? Not at all. These are intentional components of a dwelling designed to be *portable*. God wants these people to follow in Abraham's footsteps and *move with him*. Geographically the destination is the Promised Land, but more specially the direction is always straight into his presence. Follow the cloud. Pack up the tent. Carry the Ark.

Walk with God.

Deal or no deal

It takes 40 days for Moses to receive all the details of this heavenly download. The problem? The Israelites waiting at the foot of the mountain have not yet been formed in patient trust. They start to get anxious, fickle and demanding in Moses' absence. Astonishingly and heartbreakingly, only 40 days after they made a covenant with God, they ask Aaron to give them another leader and make them gods to go before them.

God knows something has gone wrong and instructs Moses to get back down to the people and tell them God is finished with them. Angry and heartbroken, God has had enough. Like he did with Noah, only this time without a flood, God is ready to start again with Moses. Once again God himself is caught up in a drama of rejection.

God's dilemma this time, though, is that he has found a partner who won't let go of him or his dream! Incredibly, Moses has started to feel the same way God does about his people. God is angry at the Israelites' staggering act of betrayal, but Moses knows God well enough by now to know that beneath his anger, God is still unfailing and steadfast in his Love. Moses appeals to God's own heart. 'Turn from your fierce anger; relent and do not bring disaster on your people.'[28] As God hears the echo of his own heart in Moses' words, his response is summed up in these remarkable words: 'The LORD relented.'[29]

God decides not to punish the people as he said he would. But what will he do now? He will allow them to go up into the Promised Land but he has decided he can't go with them. They will have to go alone. As the narrative continues, an awesome scene unfolds . . .

Moses goes out to meet with God in the tent of meeting. The people wait at their own tents, with bated breath. What will become of Moses? What will become of them? What deal might Moses make with God on their behalf? For Moses, the thought of God not going with them is unbearable. His response leads us into another sacred moment in Scripture. 'Then Moses said to him, "If your Presence does not go with us, do not send us up from here."'[30] A holy stand-off ensues. Metaphorically speaking, Moses has just pushed all his chips into the middle of the table, stared into God's face and said, 'I'm all in – I'm not going anywhere without you.'

One can only imagine the holy hush in heaven. Moses wants assurance that God is going with them. God is undone. Moses has got it. Really got it. More than any promise God could ever give, Moses wants the Presence.

God can't hide his delight with Moses: 'And the LORD said to Moses, "I will do the very thing you have asked, because I am pleased with you and I know you by name."'[31]

A risky request

Realizing he has touched a deep and tender place in the heart of God, Moses dares to ask for more. 'Show me your glory.'[32]

Like a father whose heart has been captivated by a beloved child, God bends to Moses' request, but only in a way that will not harm him. For Moses cannot see the fullness of God's glory or he will die. God, however, will respond to this risky request in one of the clearest unveilings of his essence and nature in all of history. Moses readies himself in the rock face of Mount Sinai and God descends in a cloud.

God proclaims his Name: *Yahweh, Yahweh*. Moses can connect the Name to where it all began for him: the burning bush. But this time, from the cloud, God says more:

. . . the compassionate and gracious God, slow to anger, abounding in love and faithfulness, maintaining love to thousands, and forgiving wickedness, rebellion and sin. Yet he does not leave the guilty unpunished; he punishes the children and their children for the sin of the parents to the third and fourth generation.[33]

As Moses experiences the exquisite purity of the nature of God, he bows his head in worship and his face literally lights up with the glory of God.

Missing out

The remaining chapters of Exodus, along with the books of Leviticus, Numbers and Deuteronomy, tell of the rest of the Israelites' wilderness wanderings. After one year of intense drama around Mount Sinai the cloud lifts and the Israelites begin to move towards the Promised Land. The wilderness journey is important but it was never the end goal. A great inheritance awaits.

Moses sends 12 spies ahead of the people to check out the land of their destination. Just as God said it would be, this work of espionage confirms a good land flowing with milk and honey.[34] Two of the spies, Joshua and Caleb, bring a faith-filled report of hope for all that lies ahead. But the other ten spies, while acknowledging how good the land is, focus on the fact that the land is beset with giants. On hearing this report the people are gripped by fear and complaints once again rise up. Despite God's miraculous deliverance and continuous provision for them during their first year in the wilderness, the Israelites have not learned to trust God. God can no longer partner with their lack of faith and rebellious spirit. They have known a great deliverance, but they have forfeited their inheritance. And so, a journey which was supposed to take 40 days will become a wandering of 40 years. God must wait for a new generation to emerge.

Man on fire

It will be another 38 years before this new generation will be ready to cross into the Promised Land.[35] Moses leads them all these years. Israel's wilderness account is concluded by his passionate preaching to the new generation. This is the core substance of the book of Deuteronomy. God spoke to Moses through a bush on fire and to the freed slaves from a mountain on fire. This time God's words of destiny and promise flow from the mouth of a *man* on fire. Moses, now in his final days, will preach his heart out, reminding the people of the great story their lives have been caught up in. He exhorts them to hold fast to the terms of the covenant. Walk with Yahweh. Choose life. Obey the voice of the Lord and blessing will overtake you. Disobey and you will invite devastating ruin upon your lives. Seize your inheritance.

Moses himself will not be allowed to enter the Promised Land. Like his forefathers, Abraham, Isaac and Jacob, Moses has made mistakes. His disobedience has severe consequences for him and for others. Yet, in experiencing God's forgiveness, Moses has learned how to grow old with God in sweet and enduring friendship. God himself has become Moses' Promised Land. God will bury his friend in Moab.[36]

As the meekest human in all the earth takes his last breath, a nation has been born.

From the origins of a small nomadic tribe God has formed a covenant people under his loving rule. Abraham's descendants now have a story of rescue and liberation from slavery to carry with them and their children. Forged in the wilderness and affirmed as God's treasured possession, a great inheritance awaits them.

But they must learn from their mistakes if they are to be the people through whom the Eternal Family's divine desire will bring blessing to all the earth.

Presence: God's promise of his presence has not failed Abraham's descendants 400 years later when they are bound up in slavery in Egypt. God 'comes down' to lead the slaves out and into destiny. His presence – a cloud by day and fire by night – will guide them into their inheritance. God has plans for them beyond what they can imagine, but they must learn his presence is their ultimate inheritance. God confirms this through the instructions of the tabernacle. He wants to dwell among them. But the Israelites don't really get it. Except Moses. He knows God's presence alone is what sets them apart. 'If you do not go with us, do not send us up from here.' God is undone. Moses' actions have revealed the essence of the plot. God wants to be one with us.

Family: God brings the Hebrew slaves out of the harsh reality of Egyptian authoritarian rule to form them into a loving family. This will not be easy but God will not settle for less. God will call them his own treasured possession, shaping them into a society that looks like the Eternal Family. God's commandments to bring order to their community life will carry vertical and horizontal dimensions because God wants his family to love him and to overflow with love for one another.

Kingdom: The power-hungry empire of Egypt is the antithesis of the kingdom of God. God dismantles the unjust systems of the empire to reveal his loving reign based on justice and compassion for all. He is making the former despised slaves into a kingdom of priests and a holy nation – a people who will connect the beauty of heaven to the brokenness of earth. God wants this community to showcase his purposes to the nations so the whole earth will be filled with his loving reign.

Father, thank you that you liberate us into freedom where you want to dwell among us. Help us, like Moses, to settle for nothing less than your presence. Help us to love you above all else and love our neighbours so we can help connect heaven to earth.

5

The Rise and Fall of the Kingdom of Israel

'Moses is dead.' An abrupt start to introduce the next chapter of The God Story!

God has granted time for the Israelites to grieve the father of their nation, but equally God will not allow their sorrow to be prolonged. The past is to be grieved and honoured but not sentimentalized. God is living this story with his people and it is time for a new generation to turn the page and step into the next part of the drama. Forty days after their great leader has died, his young apprentice faces the most defining moment of his life.

Joshua – stepping up with courage

'Now therefore arise . . .'[1]

Discerning a major transition while dealing with grief is a tricky process for any of us. Leading a whole people through a time of national mourning and uncertainty will need another level of courageous leadership entirely. Joshua is the chosen one.

Despite the gifts Joshua possesses it is important to note the real secret of his success. When God met powerfully with Moses in Exodus 33, Joshua was given some degree of access to the encounter between Yahweh and Moses: 'The LORD would speak to Moses face to face, as one speaks to a friend. Then Moses would return to the camp, but his young aide Joshua son of Nun did not leave the tent.'[2]

Notice how this astonishing text points to the defining mark of Moses' successor. When Moses left, Joshua 'did not leave the tent'. The young apprentice lingered in God's presence not because Moses told him to but because he had tasted God's goodness himself and now he wanted more.

The hopes and dreams of a generation may rest squarely on his shoulders yet Joshua knows if he has the presence of God, anything is possible. Joshua has been formed in the presence of God, the key qualifying characteristic of any leader called to lead others into new frontiers of spiritual destiny. God assures Joshua of his presence: 'As I was with Moses, so I will be with you; I will never leave you nor forsake you.'[3]

Joshua's willing partnership matters. Every generation needs young women and men to step up when their spiritual mothers and fathers die. Joshua steadies himself, silences his insecurities, trusts what (who) he carries and leads out with the words of Yahweh ringing in his ears, 'Be strong and courageous, because you will lead these people to inherit the land I swore to their ancestors to give them.'[4] Three times God says, 'be strong and courageous.' Courage will be needed. God will give it to Joshua. This is the moment to walk in the footsteps of Abraham, Isaac, Jacob and Moses.

Joshua's first leadership task is a proverbial baptism of fire. He is to prepare the people to cross the River Jordan. This generation has heard the stories of the Red Sea, but 40 years later God will grant them an opportunity for their own miracle story. Joshua asks the people to consecrate themselves for three days and then they begin to move. This time a cloud will not lead them; the Ark of the Covenant will. The Ark, which now represents the locus of the presence of God on the earth, will go first, lifted high on poles by the priests. The method may be different, but the principle is the same: prioritize the presence of God. Then, the priests are instructed to put their feet in the water; only ruthless trust in God can unlock the inheritance he has destined for them. As they do, Ark held aloft, the waters begin to recede. What happens next is noteworthy: 'the waters coming down from above stood and rose up in a heap very far away'.[5] God is working miles upstream, beyond and outside what the Israelites can naturally see, yet it is their act of faith that brings the sovereign purposes of God into view. Interestingly we are told these waters are stacked up as far back as the city of *Adam*. Is this a wordplay? A tip of the hat to the reality that God has already begun the process of redeeming it all – all the way back to the moment Adam and Eve disobeyed.

Gilgal

The children of Israel walk through the river on dry land. After more than 400 years of waiting, they place their feet on the Promised Land. If Egypt was 'the land of not enough' and the wilderness 'the land of just enough', Canaan (the Promised Land) represents 'the land of more than enough' – overflowing abundance! But in order to truly access their inheritance, this new generation needs to be reminded of their identity and vocation. Without a living memory of the legacy they are standing in, they will be in danger of being disconnected from The God Story that makes sense of their lives. Gilgal will be an important first step for this new generation in the Promised Land.

The elation of the Jordan crossing quickly subsides when news spreads throughout the camp at Gilgal that all the males are to be circumcised, the physical sign of the covenant Yahweh made with his people. Alongside the act of circumcision Joshua leads the people in a Passover meal, celebrating how God freed their parents from the evil regime of Egypt. These identity-affirming practices re-story the imaginations of the new generation. The fact that this happens at a place God named Gilgal is not insignificant:

> Then the LORD said to Joshua, 'Today I have rolled away the reproach of Egypt from you.' So the place has been called Gilgal to this day.[6]

Gilgal means literally 'rolling'. The God who covered the shame of Adam and Eve in the Garden of Eden is now rolling away the shame (reproach) the Israelites have carried for centuries. God released their mothers and fathers from the actual chains of slavery. Now he is freeing them from the stigma, false labels and generational curses still following them around. Gilgal marks a new day for a new generation. The narrative also goes on to reveal how the wilderness manna would stop at Gilgal, where 'they ate the produce of Canaan'.[7] God is teaching this new generation how to feed themselves, how to grow in maturity and the authority required to steward the dream of God. We all need a Gilgal.

Are you for us or against us?

The first of the battles which lie ahead for the Israelites in the Promised Land is for the intimidating fortress of Jericho. As Joshua contemplates the Israelites' strategy to get behind the impenetrable walls of Jericho, the narrative reveals how an impressive soldier with a drawn sword appears from nowhere before him. Joshua can only think to ask him, 'Are you for us or for our enemies?'[8] The response is striking: 'Neither.' What? Talk about dodging the question. The rest of the soldier's response, however, is emphatic: '. . . but as commander of the army of the LORD I have now come.'[9] Joshua, now realizing this is no ordinary commander, falls down before him. This is Joshua's own burning bush moment. 'The commander of the LORD's army replied, "Take off your sandals, for the place where you are standing is holy."'[10]

This heavenly Soldier has appeared to remind Joshua that God is beyond the tribal gods and any of our own personal political purposes. God will not allow us to use his name to simply prop up our own ideology. God is not 'for us' any more than he is for 'our enemies'. Joshua must remember that to be elected and known as God's people comes with great responsibility: to serve God's sovereign purposes and not our own. We are to posture ourselves humbly under the presence of God, like the Israelites who marched out towards Jericho, carrying the Ark of the Covenant on their shoulders. The way to see the walls of the enemy come down is a mixture of worship, humility and obedience, an opposite spirit to the opposing kingdoms of this world.

Jericho's walls will fall, as will many other subsequent strongholds in Canaan, but the core components of these victories are always the humble stewardship of the presence of God and obedience to his voice. Joshua makes it clear that they have not been granted the land for personal privilege but to populate it with the culture of God's loving rule and reign. Ultimately Joshua renews the covenant, passionately charging the people, 'Choose for yourselves this day whom you will serve'.[11] He echoes the words of Moses at Mount Sinai, calling them to hold fast to the Lord; to be uncompromising in their love for God and to 'throw away the foreign gods'.[12]

Joshua's life ends on a positive note. 'Israel served the LORD throughout the lifetime of Joshua and of the elders who outlived him.'[13] God is faithful to his promises.[14] Perhaps this new generation could fulfil the vocation of a 'holy nation' under God?

Judges: a dark repeating cycle

The hopes we carry with us at the end of the book of Joshua are quickly dashed as we turn to the first pages of Judges. Tragically we are told:

> another generation grew up who knew neither the LORD nor what he had done for Israel. Then the Israelites did evil in the eyes of the LORD and served the Baals. They forsook the LORD, the God of their ancestors, who had brought them out of Egypt.[15]

Another rupture in the plotline has taken place. The God who has always longed to be known is now completely unknown by a generation who have disconnected themselves from their story. As such, the Judges narrative spanning 300 years is characterized by a dark repeating cycle:

Idolatry → Judgement and oppression → Repentance → Deliverance → Repeat cycle

In rejecting their divine vocation and turning to worship idols, the Israelites invite judgement on their lives. This judgement is experienced in the form of oppression from their enemies. In their distress the people cry out in repentance, acknowledging they have sinned, and ask God for mercy. Moved with compassion God grants deliverance in the form of judges, raising up men and women who will lead them into freedom. But the Israelites have short memories. Like self-obsessed children who never grow up, every time the Lord brings about a deliverance for them, they continue to return to their own ways, each time even more corrupt than the generation before.[16]

There are 13 Judges altogether. Their lives and exploits, particularly those of Deborah, Gideon and Samson (that guy went wild with the jawbone of a donkey!),[17] make for memorable bedtime stories. Yet despite the supernatural ways God uses them, scratch beneath the surface and you will find most of them aren't that impressive. Nevertheless, God keeps weaving his story of salvation through them. God uses unlikely, imperfect rascals like us. Sigh of relief!

As the book of Judges ends, the increasing levels of corruption have escalated to an unthinkably dark place. Israel is in a bad, bad way. A civil war has broken out which results in increasing division among the 12 tribes of Israel. In the closing chapters of Judges a heartbreaking summary of Israel's lowest point is recorded twice: 'In those days Israel had no king; everyone did as they saw fit.'[18] What a tragic description of where humanity's pride and sinful self-reliance will ultimately lead. The dark cycle we see in the period of the Judges points to the even bigger circle of a rebellious humanity spiralling out of control since the Fall.

This depressing end to Judges is echoed in some of the early words of the book of 1 Samuel: 'the word of the LORD was rare; there were not many visions.'[19] On the surface of things, it seems the plot has completely unravelled. Once again, The God Story requires a willing partner at a threshold moment in the narrative. Step forward another heroine, another barren woman God can trust.

Hannah and Samuel: a new era

Hannah, despite the heartbreak of her infertility, is a woman who loves the presence of God. We open 1 Samuel to find her in the midst of grief, shame and pain, pouring out her longing to the Lord.[20] Hannah asks the Lord to give her a son, promising to dedicate him to the service of the Lord all the days of his life. Hannah's genuine surrender becomes a receptacle for the dreams of God. God grants Hannah the desire of her heart. The story of God will be catapulted forward again through the prayer of a barren woman. As we will see in the chapters ahead, Israel will soon experience the best days of its nation's history, and it's important we trace these glory days back to this broken-hearted but fully surrendered woman, pouring out her soul to the Lord. Hannah demonstrates how our 'broken hallelujahs' when offered up to God can be transformed into songs of joy that bring to birth the purposes of God in the world.

Samuel is born into this moment of religious apathy and spiritual malaise. And, when the time is right, Hannah brings her boy to the temple. Samuel's innocence and hunger for the presence of God are presented in stark contrast to the negligence and compromise of the existing priesthood. Eli, the high priest, has become lax and irresponsible in his old age. His sons are downright corrupt. In comparison, Hannah's faithfulness has formed in Samuel a love for the presence of God. Even though he doesn't understand it, he is captured by it: 'Samuel ministered before the LORD . . . Samuel was lying down in the house of the LORD, where the ark of God was.'[21] Samuel's proximity to the presence of God is the context for a beautiful moment. God speaks Samuel's name; a voice so familiar yet Samuel doesn't recognize it. But God hears a captivating tone of availability in the young boy's voice. 'Here I am,' Samuel replies. God calls again. And again. Three times God calls Samuel's name. Three times Samuel thinks it's Eli. Samuel's ears are about to be tuned to the frequency of heaven, but first Eli has to come to terms with the fact that his days as God's oracle to Israel have come to an end. God is going to have to bypass the existing institution which has become stale and callous.

Picture Eli – in all the magnificence of his priestly regalia alongside the boy Samuel dressed in a simple linen tunic, a mere intern in the temple. Yet it's the contrast in posture that the narrative wants to highlight. Samuel is 'lying down in the house of the LORD, where the ark of God was'. Eli has lost his first love. God has responded to Samuel's posture of hunger and humility. Anything can happen now.

Samuel hears his name a fourth time and his availability is now matched by expectancy. 'Speak, for your servant is listening,' Samuel replies. God speaks a word that will change Israel's trajectory as a nation: 'I am about to do something in Israel that will make the ears of everyone who hears about it tingle.'[22] Eli's time is up. Something new is coming which is going to shake everyone up.

In the days ahead, Samuel will lead Israel as the last of the judges and the first of the prophets. Samuel's life serves as a bridge into a new era of The God Story. His obedience to God fills the vacuum of authentic spiritual leadership which has existed within Israel's national life. Samuel brings reform, calling the people to repentance, leading them in victory over the Philistines and restoring worship, ushering in a time of peace within Israel's borders.

But the new thing God has done through Samuel isn't enough for the people of Israel. Old patterns return and once again they are seduced by other gods. By this stage, though, Samuel is near the end of his life and the people don't trust his corrupt sons to rule. The alternative suggestion is even worse. Like the Canaanite cities surrounding, the people cry out their desire for a king. Samuel is crushed by this request. God's response to Samuel is characterized by heartbroken resignation: 'it is not you they have rejected, but they have rejected me.'[23]

Plan B

This is a defining moment in The God Story. 'Plan A' for God has always been to rule with his people.[24] This is what constituting Israel as a kingdom of priests has been about; *all of Israel would rule with God*, together they would carry his dream for the world.

Devastatingly, his people express their preference for a system of rule just like their pagan neighbours had. Now one man alone will rule over them. Called to be 'set apart' from the other nations, the Israelites now tragically want to be like them. God will grant them their wish, but make no mistake, this was never God's best. Cue 'Plan B' – a concession but never the ideal. God in his kindness will continue to live this story with the Israelites and bless them if the king and the people honour him. But God makes clear the potential these human kings have for selfish gain and the terrible consequences that could follow. Nevertheless, the people will have their wish. A dramatic shift is taking place. Israel is transitioning into a recognized monarchy.

Saul: what could have been?

God graciously orchestrates things so the new monarchy can get off to the best possible start. If the people want a king, God will give them a good one. Saul, anointed by Samuel, is accomplished, impressive and gifted. God has placed his Spirit upon Saul but Saul has a choice to make: will he be a willing partner and walk with God? Things start well for Saul but his role in The God Story becomes one of the greatest 'what might have been' tales ever told. For all his qualities, Saul has a 'divided heart'. He obeys halfway. He is insecure. He seeks the acclaim of the people too much. He presumes his position at the top of the hierarchy can validate his self-centred decisions, and seeks to justify himself even when he is proven wrong. Deflecting responsibility, he becomes a master of the Blame Game. Maybe Samuel could have mentored Saul better, but ultimately Saul hasn't allowed himself to be truly 'formed' in the presence of God, and the fault lines deep in the structure of his identity come to the surface in the form of jealousy, pride and competitiveness. With these motives driving his decision-making, in the end Saul commits an act of outright disobedience. Samuel informs Saul that God has had enough. The kingdom will be ripped from Saul's hands. Like the children of Israel in the wilderness, he will miss out on a glorious inheritance. The magnitude of what Saul has lost cannot be overstated. God has made clear an everlasting kingdom could have one day come through Saul if he had obeyed. The promise will now be passed on to another, one with a heart after God.

David: a heart after God

Samuel is left to grieve the failure of Saul, but God's search for a new king has already started:

> The LORD said to Samuel, 'How long will you mourn for Saul, since I have rejected him as king over Israel? Fill your horn with oil and be on your way; I am sending you to Jesse of Bethlehem. I have chosen one of his sons to be king.'[25]

Something subversive is happening. A new king is about to be anointed while the existing one is still in position. The zeal of the Lord is burning. God wants his people to have a king who will reflect God's loving reign, one with a heart after his own.[26] God directs Samuel to Bethlehem and the house of Jesse. Samuel is initially spoiled for choice. Jesse's seven sons are all, on the face of things, more than suitable candidates for the kingship. Samuel is particularly drawn to Eliab, the oldest. He looks like he has all the attributes, but God reminds Samuel, 'Do not consider his appearance or his height, for I have rejected him. The LORD does not look at the things people look at. People look at the outward appearance, but the LORD looks at the heart.'[27]

Samuel works his way through the other brothers. No divine green light is granted. Samuel is flummoxed. He asks Jesse, eh . . . are there any more?

'There is still the youngest,'[28] Jesse replies, 'who is out in the fields,' which is code for, 'Frankly we didn't even think to include him.' Samuel asks for the boy to be brought in. As David enters the house the Lord speaks, clearly and definitively, 'Rise and anoint him; this is the one.'[29] God has got his man. David is anointed by the old prophet and the Spirit of the Lord will rest on him from this moment on.

Directly after David's profound moment of anointing there seems to be little change. Saul is still on the throne and Samuel just leaves! But *something* has happened. Yahweh has bound himself to this young boy and a seed of God's dream for the world has been planted in David's heart. One might expect the narrative to focus more on the details of Saul's continued reign at this point in Israel's story. Yet it is the character, gifts and personality of David that The God Story is most interested in.

Through the rest of 1 Samuel we read of a shepherd boy faithfully looking after the sheep, a skilled and anointed musician who can dispel evil spirits through his harp and, perhaps most famously, a mighty young warrior capable of not only protecting sheep but also slaying giants. As David's prominence rises, so does Saul's jealousy. David will have to go into hiding, a fugitive on the run. He will spend most of his twenties in a crucible of formation. The long years between anointing and appointing are significant. Undergoing intense integrity tests, in obscurity and hiddenness, prepares him for all that lies ahead. Once again God is doing his work in the wilderness. This is David's seminary, his hard-knock school of training in righteousness. But the call of leadership follows David to the wilderness. He is presented as a man of the people. A leader who empowers discontented and distressed men to become an integral part of his army who will serve alongside him for the rest of his life.

In 2 Samuel the focus on David's life continues but a shift takes place. Saul dies and David eventually ascends to the throne at 37 years old. 2 Samuel's account of David's kingship reads like a modern-day political thriller. The narrative is an enthralling cocktail of skilled leadership, political manoeuvring, succession conspiracies, sexual scandals, courtroom cover-ups. David's accomplishments, of which there are many, are clearly laid out, as are some shocking moments of failure. During all this, what shine through strongest are David's security in God's love and his passionate pursuit of God's presence. We know this not just from Samuel's narrative but also through the many poems and prayers David contributed to the Psalms. Here we witness a soul laid bare before God. David's whole life – the good, the bad and the ugly – is offered up before God in prayer, beautifully demonstrating our original design to commune with God.

As David articulates the longings of his soul, spilling out his innermost emotions and prayers before the Lord, he provides a liturgy for image-bearing sons and daughters to sing and declare the story of God. In the psalms, we can hear the cadence of Edenic rhyme, love-songs rising up from a beloved son who is revelling in divine desire and the longing love of God. 'I remain confident of this: I will see the goodness of the Lord in the land of the living.'[30]

One thing I have desired

Placing David's psalms alongside Samuel's narrative of his life helps us discover the secret of David's rise to become Israel's greatest ever leader. His passionate pursuit of God's presence has unlocked the blessings of God on his life and those he leads. David is a living example of what God's promise to Abraham, made fourteen generations before, was all about. David lives in the blessing of God and this blessing overflows into his own people, provoking jealousy within the surrounding nations. The rise of Israel as a leading nation and the legacy of Israel's glory days will be forever bound up in his extraordinary reign as king. Yet the primary factor in David's rise to power is not his military prowess, his charismatic personality or his strategic brilliance. It all comes back to one thing for David. One thing alone:

> One *thing* I have desired of the Lord,
> That will I seek:
> That I may dwell in the house of the Lord
> All the days of my life,
> To behold the beauty of the Lord,
> And to inquire in His temple.[31]

David's all-consuming desire for God is the core motivating force of his life: 'You, God, are my God, earnestly I seek you; I thirst for you, my whole being longs for you . . . Because your love is better than life, my lips will glorify you.[32]

Even through the mistakes, disappointments and regrets of his life, David finds a way to keep his heart soft before the Lord. He invites God to search his whole being, to form truth in the deep places of his soul, to give him 'an undivided heart'.

A home for God and a king forever

The testimony of David's wholeheartedness throughout his lifetime is reflected in perhaps his greatest accomplishment: establishing a culture of worship and 'presence' at the centre of Israel's national life. 2 Samuel 5—7 tells us after David makes Jerusalem his home, he makes a decision to bring the Ark of the Covenant to the city. Like Moses on Mount Sinai, David knows that without the presence of God Israel would be indistinguishable from any other pagan nation. The Ark of the Covenant has been hidden for years. It is now time to bring it back home.

The Ark's pilgrimage to Jerusalem is a painful one, though. God allows one of David's men to die after touching the Ark when it seems it might fall. At first glance this seems like a serious overreaction from God, but the Israelites should know the well-established pattern required to transport the Ark. Placing the Ark on a cart rather than carrying it on poles reveals a heart-posture that lacks the humility and awe stewarding the presence of God on behalf of others requires. David has a few soul-searching months. If he is going to unite a nation around the presence of God, then he will have to prepare them for what this will mean, starting with his own heart.

A few months later, David tries again. This time David's pilgrimage to bring the Ark to Jerusalem is marked by surrender, purity and celebration. The Ark finally finds a home in Jerusalem and David impressively implements a vision to order the public life of Israel around 24-7 Prayer. Israel could not be in a better place, but David is still not content. He has become uncomfortable with the thought of living in a palace while the Ark simply resides in a small tent. God's people need to properly honour God's presence.

David resolves to build God a temple.

God's response to David's desire is breathtaking. Initially God reminds David he doesn't need a palace. He's never really been that *in* to buildings as he has always moved freely with his people. At the same time God loves the holy ambition in David's heart and, like with Abraham and Moses, God hears the echo of his own heartbeat in David's request. David's heart has become one with God. He wants to build a home for God. But now God responds essentially saying, 'David, I am going to build you a home! For ever!'

> When your days are over and you rest with your ancestors, I will raise up your offspring to succeed you, your own flesh and blood, and I will establish his kingdom . . . Your house and your kingdom will endure for ever before me; your throne shall be established for ever.[33]

God's plans and purposes for humanity have been bound to David's life and legacy. To prove it God re-establishes a covenant with him. A covenant which will be fulfilled in a King who will reign forever.

Israel's decline

Astonishingly, after all this, David completely messes up. The Bible once again proves itself more honest than we are usually willing to be. He sees a woman, Bathsheba, bathing and he *wants* her. The lust of his desire supersedes his self-control. Through a shocking act of selfishness and abuse of power, David manipulates the circumstances to have her husband, Uriah, killed in battle. David takes Bathsheba as his own, thinking no one will really know the backstory. In one of the most riveting exposés in Scripture, Nathan the prophet visits David months later, to tell him God hasn't missed a thing.

David has failed big time and must bear the consequences. In fact, despite the hero status attached to David's kingship, in the chapters that follow a rather tragic end to his reign is revealed. He has led a great nation but his flaws meant he couldn't lead his own household, triggering all sorts of succession problems.

That being said, David repents in godly sorrow and grief over his affair with Bathsheba, crying out to God in desperation: 'Create in me a pure heart.'[34] God is attracted to David's humble contrition, forgives him and will not violate the covenant he made with him. In a wild act of God's mercy, David and Bathsheba will have a son called Solomon who will be assigned by God to fulfil the dream that originated in his dad's heart.

Solomon's reign could not have got off to a better start. He asks the Lord for wisdom to rule the people of God and God lavishly bestows it on him. He is not only empowered in skilled decision-making but also anointed to write outstanding pieces of literature, such as Song of Songs, Proverbs and Ecclesiastes, which are included in the 'wisdom' section of The God Story. Solomon builds Israel into a prosperous empire, the envy of all its neighbours. He also completes the construction of the temple, dedicating it unto the Lord by kneeling, and with outstretched arms he declares the promises of God over the new holy space and the people. Picture the scene as God fills the temple with the cloud of his presence so tangibly that the priests could not enter the building. The people fall face down and worship as God promises Solomon that if he stays true to the covenantal framework he could expect the same blessing bestowed upon his father David to be on him.

What could possibly go wrong? Well, tragically, almost everything. 1 Kings 11 outlines a startling pivot. Solomon's life swings in the opposite direction, away from the presence of God, and as it does he leads the nation of Israel down a depressing and tragic spiral. Part of Solomon's problem is obvious: 'King Solomon was obsessed with women.'[35] Later we read Solomon acquired up to 700 wives and 300 concubines. We know, we've tried to do the maths too and just can't figure it out!

Isn't it incredible to think that Moses warned the Israelites (Deuteronomy 17.14–20) approximately 600 years before to make sure their future kings did not take multiple wives, gain excessive silver or gold or acquire great numbers of horses? Solomon broke all three rules. Further, while Solomon completes the temple, he builds his own palace considerably bigger and spends almost twice as long building it. Solomon may love God, but he also loves himself – way too much. Solomon may want the glory of God, but he also desires the personal fame that comes with it. The root of pride, continuing to destroy image-bearers since the Fall, finds a place to grow in Solomon's heart as it is exposed to the celebrity and profile that come with leadership. Devastatingly, in the second half of Solomon's reign, Israel evolves to resemble Egypt more than Eden. We read of harems facilitating political marriages, oppressive state control in the forms of heavy taxes and slave labour and an army to protect the royal elite. Unthinkably, God's people, a nation defined by their liberation from oppression, have now become the oppressors.

A kingdom divided

God's hand of blessing upon Solomon's reign was removed and Israel's kingdom began to crumble, God soon declaring that the kingdom would be given to someone else. The only obvious successors, Jeroboam (a former commander in Solomon's court) and Rehoboam (one of Solomon's sons), were both immature and reckless, their foolish rivalry leading to the ultimate division of Israel's 12-tribe monarchy. The 10 tribes, under Jeroboam's leadership, took the territory to the north of Palestine and became known as 'The Northern Kingdom' (or 'The Kingdom of Israel'). The two remaining tribes, Judah and Benjamin, became known as 'The Southern Kingdom' (or 'The Kingdom of Judah'). The ensuing chapters of 1 Kings and 2 Kings will go on to tell the story of Israel's divided kingdom and the kings of both. The exploits of these kings make for gripping reading, but ultimately The God Story reveals almost all these kings failed to live in line with God's loving rule and reign. All of the 19 kings of the Northern Kingdom of Israel were bad and 'did evil in the eyes of the LORD'.[36] In the Southern Kingdom, of the 20 kings, 12 were bad, 6 were 'OK' and 2 stood out as kings worthy of mention. Hezekiah and Josiah led revolutionary reforms in difficult circumstances which we continue to be inspired by today. But, broadly speaking, the 500 years of Israel's story after Solomon is a sorry tale of idolatry and indulgence, ego and evil.

God had planted Israel like a new tree, in a land of promise to flourish for his glory. Joshua, the Judges, Samuel, David, even Solomon (before he blew it!) had called the people to covenant faithfulness. This would ensure the tree would grow up to be healthy and fruitful. David's reign had given them a taste of the fruit of the divine favour they could enjoy when they were aligned to God's purposes.

But they had allowed their hearts to be stolen by other gods and settled for the superfluous growth of fame and power. The glorious heights Israel attained under David's leadership had descended into the outright rebellion and wickedness of the divided kingdoms. Israel had been called to change the world, but ultimately they weren't prepared to change themselves. The mighty oak Israel had become under David had been so damaged by sin it would need to be cut down to a stump.

Only a holy seed would remain.

Presence: The rise of Israel was a result of their prioritization of God's presence; conversely, the fall of Israel was connected to a lack of honour for it. Their leaders epitomized this pattern. Joshua, Hannah, Samuel, David and Josiah were people who prioritized the presence of God and therefore stewarded God's favour, leading the people into blessing. The kings who didn't honour God's presence led the nation into perilous times. David, in all his weakness and sin, gives us glimpses into what it is to live a life longing for the presence of God above all. He built a permanent home for God, a picture of God's original dream: ongoing communion with his image-bearers.

Family: The result of Israel's rise under the favour of God was a spirit of unity among the 12 tribes, honouring one another in harmony and one-mindedness. On the other hand, when the children of Israel became self-centred and prideful, the dysfunctions in their relationships escalated into shattering division. In the second half of Solomon's reign, Israel resembled the dominating empire of Egypt more than God's loving family.

Kingdom: God had promised to give Israel a land. But God wanted them to populate it with the culture of God's kingdom. Humble obedience and trust in God were needed to see strongholds fall as they lived into their inheritance. But a major shift took place under Samuel's leadership: Israel wanted to mimic the other nations and asked for a king. God felt this rejection deeply but granted their request. God had wanted Israel to carry his loving rule together, shepherded by leaders who carried his heart.

Father, may your presence be the one thing we desire. Help us to understand the consequences of a divided heart. Forgive us when we elevate other leaders above you. We trust your good leadership to form us into a family reflecting your heart.

Questions for reflection: Despite David's devastating moral failure and weaknesses, he asked God for an undivided heart. What are the sins or distractions that could divide your heart? Israel put their hope in human kings over and above God. Why do we often put our hope in other leaders rather than God? Discuss the consequences of such.

6

The Prophets and Exile

What does it feel like to peer into the aching heart of God?

Take a moment to read the words below slowly, written by the prophet Jeremiah during the decline of Israel's kingdom, communicating God's heart to his people. Notice how personal, intimate and vulnerable they are:

> I thought to myself,
>> 'I would love to treat you as my own children!'
> I wanted nothing more than to give you this beautiful land –
>> the finest possession in the world.
> I looked forward to your calling me 'Father,'
>> and I wanted you never to turn from me.
> But you have been unfaithful to me, you people of Israel![1]

Jeremiah's words remind us that the Bible is not to be read as a flat description of history but the dramatic story of how God wants his creation to know how he feels about them. Further, these words are an example of one of the primary ways God speaks to his people. Jeremiah is one of an unusual collection of men and women in the Bible, called the prophets, who help us understand what God is experiencing in his heart during the rise of Israel's monarchy and its subsequent demise.

Sixteen of these prophets wrote down what they spoke, comprising the sections from Isaiah to Malachi in our Bibles, and their significance should not be underestimated: 'For the LORD God does nothing without revealing his secret to his servants the prophets.'[2]

The prophets were not simply a mouthpiece for God. These were men and women who had personally encountered the fierce reality of the living God. Their lives were *bound up* in the burden of God's heart and they embodied the vicarious nature of his love. Rabbi Abraham Heschel argues that the source of the prophets' intense expressions and evocative language was their shared sympathy with what he calls *divine pathos* – the compassion of Yahweh.[3] Put simply, through the prophets Israel knew not only what God was saying but also what God was *feeling*. Jeremiah wept and smashed pots, Ezekiel lay on the ground and shaved his head, Hosea married and forgave a prostitute, Elijah lay on a dead body, Isaiah walked around naked. Weird? At first glance, yes! But despite their quirkiness the prophets were not over-spiritualized mystics; they were rooted in the places God's people lived, bearing witness to this truth in ways that were accessible and clear. In light of the bigger story, we begin to understand their intensity.

For the most part, God's chosen people did not want him. The prophets therefore lived in the constant heart-rending tension of God's hope for humankind and the tragedy of a world that had rejected him. And so, their words carried a dual purpose of both warning and hope. They called Israel back to covenant faithfulness, warning them of the consequences of rejecting Yahweh and his promises for their lives. They had to speak up, they had to wake the people up to the sovereign presence of God. The prophets therefore were not always popular. They wept, yelled and challenged, their words a stinging rebuke. But while they called Israel back in line with covenant faithfulness they simultaneously called God's people forward into a hopeful future. For those who were beaten down, destitute and forgotten, the prophets' words consoled and comforted. With words and pictures the prophets exhorted the people that they dare not lose hope. God would not forget his people!

Experiencing God's love as wrath

As we piece the passages of the various prophets together it becomes clear that the narrative is straining under the weight of the jealous love of God. Centuries of God's 'slow-to-anger' nature and 'abounding-in-steadfast-love' commitment have not been enough for the children of Israel to genuinely turn from their idolatrous ways. The kings of Israel have not delivered. The children of Israel have completely turned their backs on God despite the repeated warnings of the prophets. The Father's only chance of winning his people back in the long term is to let them go in the short term. Israel will experience God's love as judgement. Judgement is not something we want to talk about but, as Eugene Peterson argues, when we are talking about *God's judgement* it can never be the worst thing that can happen. God is always oriented to humanity in love. God never stops being Love. Therefore, God's actions are never to get back at us, only his consent for us to suffer the consequences of our reckless and idolatrous rebellion. This is what we call the wrath of God.[4]

Israel has invited God's judgement upon herself.

The Northern Kingdom (Israel)

Bearing the consequences of their dire choices means things are going to get worse for the children of Israel before they will get better. The people of the Northern Kingdom have constantly rebelled against God despite the warnings and supernatural phenomena of her prophets, most notably Elijah and Elisha. In a breathtaking account God tries one more time to win the ten tribes back through the life of the prophet Hosea.

God asks Hosea to marry a prostitute called Gomer as a prophetic symbol of his commitment to a nation guilty of wholesale adultery. Despite their lustful appetite for other lovers and their complete abdication of the law, God has married Israel. Tragically, Gomer will commit adultery. Hosea's words open us up to the betrayal and woundedness God is experiencing:

> Upon her children also I will have no mercy,
>   because they are children of whoredom.
> For their mother has played the whore;
>   she who conceived them has acted shamefully.
> For she said, 'I will go after my lovers.'[5]

Hurt, distraught and heartbroken, these words reveal God venting his righteous anger as he describes the Northern Israelite Kingdom's lurid and shameful exploits.

Yet halfway through the same chapter there is a sudden shift. Despite the pain, God is *still in love* with Israel. More than this, God has still imagined a reunion with Israel. We read, in some of the most breathtaking words in the whole Bible:

> Therefore, behold, I will allure her,
>   and bring her into the wilderness,
>   and speak tenderly to her.
> And there I will give her her vineyards
>   and make the Valley of Achor a door of hope.[6]

God wants Israel back. To make this clear God asks Hosea to take Gomer back despite her unfaithfulness. How do we comprehend the depths of this love? Tragically, even these tangible signs of God's unremitting love aren't enough for the Kingdom of Israel, and eventually they bring upon themselves the disastrous consequences of such outright rejection of God's ways. Hosea concludes, 'All their kings fall . . . Israel has forgotten their Maker.'[7] The Northern ten tribes which have lasted for almost 200 years fall to the ferocious and savage regime of Assyria and Tiglath-Pileser III in 720 BC. The Assyrians have a ruthless policy of leaving no remembrance of other nations. The people of the Northern Kingdom are either captured, killed or assimilated into the Assyrian Empire. Devastatingly, the ten tribes will never return.

The Southern Kingdom (Judah)

The wider geopolitical backdrop the children of Israel were living through at this point was one of increasing instability. Rival empires were flexing their muscles, yet God continued to speak directly to his people through the prophets. The Southern Kingdom were given some more time to sort themselves out. God warned the remaining two-tribe state (Judah and Benjamin) through the prophetic works of Isaiah about the fate of her Northern sister in order to sharpen her focus and obedience. 'Don't follow her example' was essentially what Isaiah was saying: 'Pledge your allegiance to God!'

Through Isaiah's admonishment and King Hezekiah's obedience, the Kingdom of Judah miraculously avoided defeat by the Assyrian army (701 BC). As alluded to in the last chapter, Hezekiah was one of only a few godly kings of the Southern Kingdom and his righteous choices allowed the Southern Kingdom to enjoy the blessings of covenant faithfulness. A handful of kings would follow Hezekiah, but apart from Josiah all of them would choose not to follow in his footsteps. Isaiah could see a similar type of oppression coming upon the Southern Kingdom because of their disobedience and he began to prophesy about the coming consequences. But it was another prophet, Jeremiah, who lived through the consequences when they eventually did come through the new superpower to emerge, Nebuchadnezzar's Babylon. Not unlike Hosea's prophetic lament regarding the Northern Kingdom's rebellion, Jeremiah presents us with an intense description of what God was experiencing on the eve of the Southern Kingdom's capture. Listen for the overwhelming agony contained in this passage:

> During the reign of King Josiah, the LORD said to me, 'Have you seen what faithless Israel has done? She has gone up on every high hill and under every spreading tree and has committed adultery there. I thought that after she had done all this she would return to me but she did not, and her unfaithful sister Judah saw it. I gave faithless Israel her certificate of divorce and sent her away because of all her adulteries. Yet I saw that her unfaithful sister Judah had no fear; she also went out and committed adultery. Because Israel's immorality mattered so little to her, she defiled the land and committed adultery with stone and wood. In spite of all this, her unfaithful sister Judah did not return to me with all her heart, but only in pretence,' declares the LORD. The LORD said to me, 'Faithless Israel is more righteous than unfaithful Judah.'[8]

Did you ever think it was possible to break God's heart like this?

Through Jeremiah we are listening to God grieving his own dream. What makes it worse is that no one listened to Jeremiah even though Judah's actions had wounded God even more deeply than their Northern neighbours had. The Southern Kingdom must also face the consequences of their wilful rebellion. The Babylonians began to raid Jerusalem. Initially the urban elites were carried off into captivity. The prophet Daniel was among those taken in the first invasion (605 BC), and in the second invasion (597 BC) it's thought that the priest Ezekiel was taken too. But it was the third invasion in 586 BC that finished off the Southern Kingdom (Judah). Nebuchadnezzar's army besieged Jerusalem, ransacked it and burnt it to the ground. Meanwhile Jeremiah, holed up in a dungeon in Jerusalem, details the grim and devastating account of just how bad it had got. The people were starved so badly that women contemplate eating their own children. Many were killed in battle, and most of the rest were carried into captivity. Only the poorest of the poor were left. The City of Zion, once the envy of the nations, was left in ruins, reduced to a miserable and dangerous outpost of the Babylonian Empire.

The lowest of the low

Picture the sad new reality. Abraham's children of promise, God's treasured possession, now find themselves completely humiliated, back in Babylon, the very place their great ancestor was called out from more than 1500 years before. Slaves to another master once again. Abraham's legacy of faith, it appears, is now left in tatters as Israel enters the darkest chapter of their existence as a nation. The Exile may not be as severe as the flood of Noah's day but it speaks to the same tragic theme of 'un-creation'. Has this all been for nothing? All the major promises contained within the covenants to Abraham, Moses and David have been stripped away. The exiles do not have land, there is no temple and their last Davidic king, Zedekiah, has been publicly blinded and bound. Can you imagine this pathetic and humiliating picture of God's people being led in chains to their captor's homeland? Significantly, Babylon is eastward.

The children of Israel have never been farther from home.

In pure historical terms, it is a marvel that Israel survives. One small mercy for those captured from the tribe of Judah is that the Babylonians are not quite as brutal as the Assyrians. While in forced subjection to the Babylonian regime, the Jews are given a degree of freedom to live and work in the hope they will eventually assimilate into the surrounding culture. The seed has not disappeared completely, but the story is hanging by a thread.

Deconstruction / reconstruction

How on earth did Israel survive? Believe it or not, it was her faith. Faced with foundational questions of survival and a crisis of identity and theology, for the children of Israel Babylon became the birthplace of a resurgent and renewed faith. For years God's people had rested on their laurels and rejected the warnings of the prophets. Surely God would always deliver them no matter what? Now this generation had to ask some big questions: Is this the death of Yahweh? What happened to his promises? Are we not supposed to always have a Davidic king on the throne?

Exile was an emergency of faith. But the Israelites learned that the questions we ask in such times *reveal* us in a way no other season does. The projections we have placed upon God are exposed. The false identities we have become attached to are laid bare. The disappointment that God didn't come through as we thought he would rises to the surface. How do we get through such seasons? How did the exiled Israelites?

Lament! The children of Israel sat by the rivers of Babylon and wept, pouring out their questions, grief and anguish to the Lord. The book of Lamentations and portions of the Psalms reveal how the exiles understood their grief and questions had to be prayed! Their pain could only be transformed if they offered it up before the face of God.

Exile for the children of Israel would become the place of recon-structed faith but only, as the prophets told, after a healthy period of deconstruction had taken place. Any hope that God would one day rescue Israel from exile was connected to an acknowledge-ment that *God had allowed this time of exile to happen*. When other nations were captured by aggressive empires, it was simply assumed their gods died with them. Jeremiah and his prophetic friends were declaring that Israel's God was different. God was not dead in exile but in fact had *sent them into exile*. Further, he would be with them in exile! Israel needed to acknowledge the part they had played in their new reality; the learning from this process would provide the foundations upon which they could rebuild.

Reconstruction would come if they trusted the process. Jeremiah's words, 'I . . . will bring you back to the place from which I carried you into exile,'[9] offered this hope. Israel had not acted as God's children should. They were experiencing God's wrath as purifying love. But they were still his children, the apple of his eye. In Babylon, stripped of everything, God was reconstructing his treasured possession.

The remnant – Daniel

Everyone has to go through seasons of exile, but not everyone walks faithfully with God through them. Like the children of Israel in the wilderness before them, many Israelites in exile gave up, surrendering to the dominant narrative of Babylon. Only a small group faithfully journey through the work of repentance referred to above. The God Story refers to this group of people as a 'remnant' – a concentrated core group of faithful people who held on to the promises of God despite the circumstances surrounding them.

One outstanding example of this remnant is Daniel. Placed right into the heart of the Babylonian royal court because of his obvious potential to enhance the rule of Babylon, Daniel 'resolved not to defile himself'.[10] Along with his three friends, Daniel coura-geously and consciously chose not to assimilate into the empire's temptations of power and prestige. Daniel would not compromise and in this way he is a paragon of radical discipleship. Daniel knew his life was not primarily shaped by the Babylonian Empire, and so, while others sold their souls to the seductive voices of Babylon promising comfort and security, Daniel's love for God motivated a devotional life of prayer, study and fasting. This is what we call counter-formation. Rooted in a time and place characterized by the might and pomp of empire, it is this young exile who is the one who shines through as carrying the real power and authority. God would show Daniel a stunning vision of powerful empires that would come and go in the years to follow, but God's kingdom would never be destroyed.[11] Daniel's encounters with God produced a faith that silenced lions, overcame demonic principalities and confidently interpreted the dreams of kings.

Inspired by leaders like Daniel in the midst of exile, Israel slowly but surely began to rebuild the foundations of their identity. With no land, temple or civic institutions to lean on, the remnant began poring over all they had left: the Torah. A renewed vigour for the word of God reminded the exiles of their story, of the promises of God and of the implications of the covenant. Building on this foundation, Israel's three major prophets, Jeremiah, Ezekiel and Isaiah, all in different ways and at different times confirmed this hopeful future which still awaited Israel.

Jeremiah – people of Shalom

Jeremiah had wept his way through the destruction of Jerusalem and the fall of the Southern Kingdom. For the most part God had called Jeremiah to prophesy warning to the people. Yet God also used Jeremiah, during Israel's darkest hour, to communicate some of the most enduring words of hope ever written: 'For I know the plans I have for you, declares the LORD, plans for welfare and not for evil, to give you a future and a hope.'[12] It would not be easy. God had made it clear the exiles would spend 70 years in Babylon. They should prepare to settle here for the foreseeable future. Yet it would not be their end. There may have been no temple in Babylon, yet

God's presence would still find them there. God wants his people to flourish in exile:

> Seek the peace and prosperity of the city to which I have carried you into exile. Pray to the LORD for it, because if it prospers, you too will prosper.[13]

Three times in chapter 29, Jeremiah repeats one of the richest Hebrew words in the Bible, *shalom*. *Shalom*, translated 'peace' or 'welfare', speaks to the idea of *wholeness* or *completeness*. Listen for the strong echo of the harmony that existed in the Garden of Eden resounding in the meaning of *shalom*.

The implication of this verse is astonishing: God wanted the exiles to not simply survive in enemy-occupied Babylon but to thrive in it. But this is not all! God called his people to seek his *shalom* not just for themselves *but also on behalf of the pagan city of their captors*. What?! Jerusalem is lying in ruins and God wants his people to seek the peace of Babylon?! Can you imagine wanting the best for the people who have sought to destroy you, your people and all that you love? God's promise to the exiles was that even here in Babylon they could be a people distinguished by a type of blessing and flourishing that can only come from his presence. That seed of promise now buried in the womb of another pagan empire could still be activated. A colony of heaven, a reflection of the Eternal Family, will be established, even here in darkest Babylon.

Ezekiel – a river of life

Unlike Jeremiah, who had been imprisoned through the initial invasions of the Babylonians, Ezekiel was deported with the other children of Israel. Ezekiel, a young 30-year-old priest, found himself among a large section of captives who had been relocated along a great canal flowing from the River Euphrates. The 'Rivers of Babylon', a place of weeping for the exiles, had become a place of revelation for Ezekiel. 'The heavens were opened and I saw visions of God.'[14]

Over the next 20 years, Ezekiel declared what the Lord showed him to the beaten-down exiles, describing the purposes of God in unforgettable and evocative imagery. His Spirit-inspired scenes not only helped pierce the despair and denial calcifying the Israelites' hearts but they also provided a theological grid for the children of Israel to reconfigure how God was still at work among them. The valley of dead bones in Ezekiel 37 represented the thoughts of many Israelites. Their nation was dead. The promises of God seemed dead. Maybe even Yahweh was dead with them. Yet something new was happening in this godforsaken valley. An army of God, filled with God's own breath, was starting to rise up.

Perhaps most striking of all, though, was Ezekiel's vision of a temple overflowing with water, running towards the east.[15] The picture of a temple would have pressed all sorts of buttons for these exiles, captive in a land far from the building that represented so much of their history and future promises. Within the temple vision a distinctive Man called out to Ezekiel, 'Son of man, have you had a good look?'[16]

Three things about this particular temple were striking.

First, the river flowed east.[17] Humankind had been moving eastward, away from the presence of God, since the beginning. Exile was the furthest east the nation of Israel had ever been. Think about the incredible encouragement it would have been to the exiles to know that, even though they had no temple in Babylon, a river of God's presence was flowing in their direction. More broadly, think about how this vision was a sign that God's redemptive Spirit was flowing like a river to all who had found themselves far from home, east of Eden.

Second, in Ezekiel's vision the water was running out the door of the temple. As it ran away from the temple the river got deeper and deeper. This would have been as strange to Ezekiel as it is to us today. Naturally, the volume of water running away from its source decreases the further away it flows. But God's presence was not in short supply. The presence of God was not just flowing eastward but it was increasing in volume and intensity as it made its way towards the children of Israel. Also, they had been taught to *go to the temple* where the glorious presence of God rested. The temple was the place to go to get away from unclean, dead things; the place to 'get holy'. In Ezekiel's vision, though, the river was not rationed exclusively to those who would go to the temple but rather was *flowing indiscriminately away from* the temple.

Third, and perhaps the most striking thing about Ezekiel's vision, was that the river brought life everywhere it flowed, even the Dead Sea! 'So where the river flows everything will live.'[18] The Dead Sea was 1400 ft below sea level and the place where every other mineral from the surrounding mountains and plains flowed into. The Dead Sea was the place where nothing lived, because nothing could live there! Everyone hearing Ezekiel's vision would have been shocked by this picture of the Dead Sea being transformed into a thriving ecosystem. But if the exiles could understand that the river flowing from the temple was carrying something much more potent than the properties of death the Dead Sea represented then they could grasp more fully what God's intention had always been for them. God's holy presence was not something that needed to be protected in a building but was a healing-agent of change which could be released into the brokenness of the world. Ezekiel's vision was teaching Israel that God's greater intention for his people was not to simply *go to the temple* but to *embody the principles of the temple*. In all the dead places of this world.

Isaiah – a light to the nations

The theme of hope and restoration heard in the prophetic words of Jeremiah and Ezekiel was confirmed emphatically through the prophetic book of Isaiah. Isaiah's name means 'God saves' and the Spirit-inspired words on the pages of his book reveal God's salvation in a way that still awakens hearts today. To read Isaiah, particularly chapters 40—55, 'is to feel one transported into a different universe, and indeed that is exactly what is happening.'[18] For Isaiah had been caught up with God and heard the divine announcement: God was coming to deliver his people.

With vivid and startling language Isaiah defibrillated the hearts of the weary exiles. Masterfully and poetically, he described the infiniteness and incomparable nature of Yahweh, yet with equal passion and spellbinding prose revealed how God was coming gently and tenderly to his flock again:

> A Message from the high and towering God,
>   who lives in Eternity,
>   whose name is Holy:
> 'I live in the high and holy places,
>   but also with the low-spirited, the spirit-crushed.
> And what I do is put new spirit in them,
>   get them up and on their feet again.'[20]

Isaiah's hopeful prose pointed to a mighty deliverance. God was going to bring his people home. Part of this deliverance Isaiah prophesied would come through another pagan empire, the Persians under Cyrus' rule. But even more significantly this restoration was pointing not simply towards immediate Jewish deliverance but to long-term redemption of the Gentiles. The promises of old to Abraham and David were being realigned through a holy remnant in exile. Isaiah wanted to remind the exiles of it:

> I will give you as a light to the nations,
>   that my salvation may reach to the end of the earth.[21]

Reflect for a moment on the astonishing nature of this hope-filled prophecy. The children of Israel, drastically reduced in number and influence through exile, are being reminded by Isaiah that they are God's light which will shine to the ends of the earth.

The new thing coming!

Each of the prophets, in their own unique way, had shed fresh light on Israel's predicament. Yet they were bound together by a common theme of newness. A close look into each prophet will reveal references to a new way, a new king, a new temple, a new creation and ultimately a new covenant. These words and pictures, pieced together, formed a prophetic mosaic of energizing hope for the children of Israel. Into the wilderness of exile God had initiated something fresh:

> Behold, I am doing a new thing;
>> now it springs forth, do you not perceive it?
> I will make a way in the wilderness
>> and rivers in the desert.[22]

The new thing coming *was a new covenant*. Jeremiah states this clearly, 'Behold, the days are coming, declares the LORD, when I will make a new covenant with the house of Israel and the house of Judah.'[23] Ezekiel backs this up but goes on to describe the unique and glorious distinction of this particular covenant that awaits God's people:

> I will give you a new heart and put a new spirit in you; I will remove from you your heart of stone and give you a heart of flesh. And I will put my Spirit in you and move you to follow my decrees and be careful to keep my laws.[24]

Isn't it incredible, scandalous even, to think that after 800 years of heartbreaking adultery, God's response to Israel, like in the Garden of Eden, is to once again bow low into the dirty mess of humanity's predicament? Only this time God promises not just to breathe his Spirit upon the remnant but to give them his very heart as well! This new covenant will involve *a more inward work of God's own Spirit*. Somehow God is going to live in them, moving them to be faithful where they never could. His law will no longer be written on tablets of stone but on their actual hearts.

The suffering servant

If Ezekiel and Jeremiah confirmed the new thing God was doing would ultimately lead to a new covenant, we must return to Isaiah's prophetic writings to understand how this new covenant would be initiated. Here, we find repeated references to a servant-type figure[25] who would undergo unthinkable suffering in order to bring about God's rule and reign. Isaiah's servant-poems carried a two-pronged interpretation. First, Israel was to embody the posture of servanthood if they were to continue to be the vessel through which God would reveal his glory to the world. Second, these words foretold One who would fully exhibit such a calling. A suffering servant would be the living instrument through which God's victory over the rulers of the world would be enacted. The promise of God would come at a price, an immeasurable and unthinkable price. But a price this suffering servant would be willing to bear.

The ideas of who this would be and how this would happen were the cause of much debate and nuance. How could God's mighty power and the meekness described in this suffering servant mash together? The general consensus was that at some point in the future a divinely inspired leader would come whose actions would be consistent with those of Yahweh himself to bring about a great deliverance. Sudden flashes of prophetic brilliance, like Zechariah's vision of a king coming on a lowly donkey, indicated this person would be a king-like figure, connected to David's throne. This servant-type leader would be different from the ones of Israel's past – those who were supposed to bring justice and peace but never did. The title given to this figure in whom Israel's hopes began to converge was 'Messiah'.

Return and rebuild

Babylon eventually crumbled before the new superpower in town, Persia. Cyrus the Great, Persia's ruler, had established his reign throughout most of what is now Western Asia. Cyrus gave Israel permission to return. Historical records show that many of the Jews gained positions of influence in Persian society and stayed! The elders of Israel's exilic remnant, however, were stirred to go back and rebuild the temple. A steady stream of Israelites followed them. One of their stand-out leaders, Zerubbabel, led the first envoy back to Jerusalem in 539 BC. Inspired by the Lord he began a restoration project for the temple. The prophets of that moment, Haggai and Zechariah, urged the people to follow Zerubbabel's lead and fulfil this project. 'Don't worry about rebuilding your own homes, build God a house first,'[26] was the core substance of the challenge they brought.

Initially, the possibility of the glory days of David and Solomon's temple being restored produced a fervour among the people towards the rebuilding project. However, as the construction process became prolonged, hope waned and tensions among the people rose. The returning exiles felt those who had remained in Jerusalem had compromised. Who really were the true descendants of David and Abraham? The initial optimism of the temple rebuilding project had dissipated and the expectations attached to Zerubbabel's initial return had not been met. Time for Nehemiah and Ezra to enter the story.

Nehemiah, who had done well in Persia, working in the royal palace, had heard about the distress in his homeland and was deeply moved by it. Carrying the burden of God, he rejected the comfort of the Persian palace and embraced the cost of God's assignment for his life. Through exceptional leadership skills, effective organization and bloody-minded defiance, Nehemiah refused to allow the city of Jerusalem to be known as a reproach. Presenting this vision in such a compelling way he was able to mobilize the families of Israel in the rebuilding project.

Nehemiah's engineering and leadership masterclass was accompanied by the gifts and authority of Ezra. If Nehemiah was God's man for the public square, Ezra was God's man for spiritual renewal. Nehemiah would rebuild the city walls; Ezra would help reform the people's hearts. Ezra rehearsed with passion and conviction Israel's sacred history and their central place in the story of God. In line with Moses, who 1000 years earlier had powerfully reminded the Israelites of their true identity, Ezra's inspired preaching bolstered a disillusioned people, anchoring their lives in the hope of the big story of salvation their destiny was tethered to. The impact was dramatic: when they heard his words they wept![27] Being reminded of their true identity, their inheritance and God's desire for them to influence the nations changed everything.

Famous last words

The years after Nehemiah and Ezra's reforms are hard to describe. On one hand the returning exiles had instilled a renewed devotion to Yahweh, but many had become dangerously obsessed with the law. On the other hand an overriding feeling of emptiness filled the air. In reality, it felt like the promises of God to their ancestors weren't being realized. They had survived exile but were still under foreign control. There was a vacuum of leadership and a growing sense of anticlimax. It's no wonder at this point the Israelites began to pore over the words of the prophets that had pointed to a deliverer. A growing expectation for a Messiah, a king who would come in the line of David, began to build among the children of Israel, embedding itself within the national psyche. But would this Messiah expectation align with the heart and purposes of God described by the prophets? Could the children of Israel understand a Messiah who was also a suffering servant, a great King who would make his way to his throne riding on a colt? To answer these questions we have to wait. Four hundred years.

The God Story plot has unravelled in ways God never intended it to. Israel has not fulfilled the glorious destiny God called it to. In many ways it looks like the narrative is meandering to a slow stop. And God is about to go quiet.

But before God does, he speaks one more word of promise through the prophet Malachi. God's famous last words reveal that the redemptive thread which has held The God Story together has not disappeared:

> See, I will send the prophet Elijah to you before that great and dreadful day of the Lord comes. He will turn the hearts of the parents to their children, and the hearts of the children to their parents; or else I will come and strike the land with total destruction.[28]

And then silence.

Presence: Even though the children of Israel continue to rebel against God, he continues to speak of his deep longing for them through the prophets, how he cannot forget them, how he will forgive them and take them back to himself. But their ongoing disobedience means God will allow his people to be carried into exile. Yet, even in exile God will find them. Ezekiel's river will remind them God's presence is flowing to them even in darkest Babylon.

Family: The tribes of Israel may have completely divided but God outlines his hope to rebuild his family in exile. *Shalom* is the word God calls the exiles to seek for their families and the city of their captors. God wants to rebuild his family on the healthy foundations of his peaceful presence. Israel will only testify to glimpses of this in the years ahead, but even before God goes silent for 400 years he will speak, through Malachi, of a future when the hearts of parents and children will be turned to one another in a beautiful promise of family unity.

Kingdom: Israel has been swallowed up by the Babylonian kingdom but a vision for God's people extending his loving rule and reign on the earth still remains. Ezekiel speaks of an army rising up from a valley of dry bones filled with the breath of God. Isaiah declares Israel will still be a light to all nations – a sure sign the seed of promise given to Abraham is still alive. Jeremiah declares even Babylon will experience God's *shalom*. The prophets declare the other kingdoms will come and go. God's *shalom* points to an everlasting kingdom.

Father, thank you that even when we are in exile your presence will find us. Help us to know the hope-filled possibilities for our lives when we are consumed with our own brokenness, pain or the consequences of our sin. May we experience your shalom *deep in our hearts and may it pulse through us to transform others with your love.*

Questions for reflection: Discuss how encouraging it is to know that God's presence flows to us even during difficult seasons. What does it look like for you in your everyday life to seek the *shalom* of your town or city?

Interlude – the Silence

We have heard God speak his desire and communicate the longing of his heart from the beginning of time, but as Eugene Peterson has taught, 'any understanding of God that doesn't take into account God's silence is a half-truth'.[1]

For 400 years after those last words of Malachi, The God Story had nothing to report. Silence. On the world stage, however, it was anything but quiet! All around Israel the noise of clashing civilizations could be heard. The contrast is stark and poignant. As the nations raged, God was quiet. As empires forcefully exerted their rule, God who rules over all was patiently waiting. As humankind shouted and screamed for power and control, God calmly rested secure in who God is!

Understanding the historical context of these 400 years is crucial to appreciating the drama that will unfold after they are completed. God's redemptive plan always has a context.

The clash of civilizations

Huge convulsions were taking place in the Ancient Near East,[2] causing intense cultural upheaval. A succession of empires were fighting it out for supremacy. The Persians who had ruled much of the Ancient Near East after Israel's return from exile were eventually defeated by the famous Macedonian, Alexander the Great, who paved the way for the Greek Empire to imprint itself on a large part of the world map. Greek language, culture and philosophy, which became known as Hellenism, had a monumental impact on civilization, and its influence is still felt in many places of the world today. The Greeks were eventually conquered by the Egyptians who in turn were defeated by the Syrians.

At this point, 167 BC, the children of Israel came under the savage rule of the infamous Syrian Antiochus Epiphanes. He defiled and desecrated the temple with the hope of crushing Jewish understanding and identity. Antiochus, however, hadn't factored in the sheer tenacity and zeal of many Jewish freedom fighters. Remarkably, a revolt led by the Jewish leader Judas Maccabeus defeated the wicked despot. This victory led the Jews into a period of independence for approximately 100 years, which many of them understood as God's vindication over their enemies. During these years the temple of Jerusalem was re-established as the epicentre of renewed nationalistic zeal. Yet while independence initially felt good, doubts surfaced, giving rise to questions. Are we really living as God's people? Is Judas Maccabeus really the Messiah? Does our reality really line up with the prophecies of Ezekiel, Jeremiah and Isaiah?

Is this the kingdom we have been waiting for?

The Roman Empire

In 63 BC the uncertainty attached to these questions was compounded when Pompey, commander of the world's new superpower, the Roman Empire, stormed the walls of Jerusalem and captured the holy city. In a further act of disdain for the Jewish religion, Pompey walked straight into the temple and into the holy of holies. At this point there was no new Judas Maccabeus capable of galvanizing the Jewish people to rise up against their oppressor. Instead, Roman rule became the new reality for the Judean region, enforced by the Roman governor Pontius Pilate. The Herodians, a sect of Hellenistic Jews, were installed by the Roman administration to give a pretence of semi-autonomy for the Jewish people. In reality, however, these rulers were simply puppets on the end of Rome's string. Herod the Great, the insane and enigmatic king we meet in the first pages of the New Testament, may have self-identified as the 'King of the Jews', but in truth this title was empty of meaning. The idea of kingship Herod embodied in Judea was a pale reflection of the Davidic-type king the prophets had foretold.

First-century Jewish worldview

This historical context helps us build a worldview of first-century Jewish life. Many people in the surrounding culture spoke Greek, dressed like Greeks and entertained in Greek ways. The Romans held the political framework of society and believed in the worship of many gods. The streets of Jerusalem were therefore filled with vestiges and reminders of pagan culture. The Jewish people had not been taken captive into foreign lands like their ancestors 500 years earlier, but now *they lived as exiles in their own land.* They were viewed by the surrounding nations as social misfits for their peculiar custom of Sabbath, their food laws and the worship of an unseen God! A typical first-century Jewish worldview was therefore built on the following thoughts: 1) we are God's chosen people who are living in the holy land but under foreign rule; 2) we are focusing on the temple even though everywhere we look we see shrines, temple-prostitutes and cultic objects of pagan gods; 3) we are subject to the wrong rulers – on one hand we are surrounded by compromised Jews, on the other we have pagan rulers and in the middle we have Herod, a self-serving narcissist who disregards God's law and sacred Jewish customs; 4) we need a deliverer.[3]

For the Jews this worldview raised many questions. How do we live distinctly from this surrounding culture? What does faithfulness to the Torah, God's instructions and law, really look like in this age? If a Messiah is coming, how should we prepare for him?

The responses to these questions among the Jews were varied, but four main streams emerged within Judaism.

Essenes: The Essenes were what we might describe as the ultimate separatists. They withdrew to the wilderness, to live in closed monk-like communities. They saw Rome's invasion of their land as punishment for not remaining faithful to the law and so became obsessed with a strict application of it. They committed themselves to lives of celibacy, working and praying all hours of the day.

Zealots: Like the Essenes, the Zealots clustered in small wilderness communities but their aim was to prepare for armed revolt against the Romans. They believed God wanted an ethnically pure

Israel and therefore a 'cleansing' role, including violence, against compromised Jews and pagan rulers was required.

Sadducees: The Sadducees were Jewish collaborators. The Romans had persuaded many Jewish influencers that it would be in everyone's interest to maintain the status quo. They could provide stability in the region while allowing a certain degree of freedom and power to be enjoyed by the Jewish elite. The Sadducees had given up on Israel's vocation as God's holy people so they were happy to provide information to the Romans concerning any kind of insurrection that might be brewing.

Pharisees: The Pharisees represented the main party of the Jewish middle class. They positioned themselves somewhere between separation and collaboration. The Pharisees were a mixture of ordinary laypeople, scribes and scholars who, for the most part, were upright people who taught the Torah. Common understandings of the Pharisees carry strong negative connotations; however, it's important to understand how devoted many Pharisees were to the Torah and their desire to see a renewal of God's law among the Jewish people. The Pharisees were less political than the Zealots and were also unconvinced by the Essenes' approach. The Pharisees believed exile had been a result of their abandonment of God's law, but different from the Essenes they wanted to apply the Torah to their current context, not simply withdraw to the desert. The problem with some of the Pharisees, however, came with their dogmatic stances on their certain interpretations of God's law, particularly laws focusing on personal cleanness, food laws and the Sabbath. This resulted in a system of legalism that created an 'insider' and 'outsider' dynamic – a religion completely at odds with the true spirit of Torah. The once genuine devotion of the remnant had, over the 400 years of silence, turned into self-righteous moralism.

A growing suspense

As each of these groups entrenched themselves deeper and deeper in their own interpretations of the law and prophecies, the tensions built. The noise of clashing civilizations surrounding Israel was juxtaposed against the amplifying echo of God's deafening silence. A suspense was building among Israel's remnant.

At this point, allow your imagination to go back to the void before creation. It seems God has entered the silence of this space once again, waiting patiently to speak another word, 'out of nothing', into being. But as Fredrick Beuchner concluded:

Before the gospel is a word it is silence.[4]

7

The Son

Four hundred years of silence were broken by the cry of a baby. The pregnancy of heaven had come full term. Longing love can be restrained no longer.

'For to us a child is born.'[1] No one thought these words uttered by the prophet Isaiah 700 years before would define the extraordinary nature of how God would decide to speak again. A whole new chapter of The God Story has opened up. The lively, talkative God of Israel who has patiently endured the longest of silences has now unmuted. A fresh intrusion of grace is coming. God himself is coming. Incognito.

'For to us a child is born.' In one way childbirth is the perfect symbol of a new beginning. Everything is new when a child is born. But as we turn the first pages of the New Testament, we come to realize it is the birth of this particular child that will impact not just his own family but also the destiny of the whole world.

How can a baby carry the hope of the nations?

Cue Matthew, Mark, Luke and John who wrote the opening books of the New Testament, known as the Gospels. In different ways these authors answer the question above by drawing together themes of The God Story. They weave together a variety of genealogies and references to Israel's past to emphasize how this child who has been born is the One the whole world has been waiting for. The great Hope the prophets spoke of has burst into the world. The whole plot has reached its climactic moment.

God will take on a human face.

Elizabeth and Zechariah

Matthew and Luke take time to describe the divinely orchestrated events that precede the birth of this child. They tell of all sorts of heavenly activity unleashed in the opening chapters of their accounts. God's messengers were delivering and releasing divine assignments to some 'unlikely' characters. There was a lack of genuine spiritual vitality within Israel but faithful ones could still be found. And God had not stopped searching for humble and contrite spirits to entrust his heart to.

A man called Zechariah was going about his normal temple duties on what appeared to be a pretty average day, when he was arrested by an angelic visitation. The angel called Gabriel told Zechariah he was going to have a son who would be a forerunner for the Messiah. As Gabriel went on to describe the destiny of Zechariah's yet-to-be-conceived son, notice the reformulation of Malachi's prophecy – the famous last words God spoke before he went quiet for 400 years:

> And he will go on before the Lord, in the spirit and power of Elijah, to turn the hearts of the parents to their children and the disobedient to the wisdom of the righteous – to make ready a people prepared for the Lord.[2]

God, it seems, was picking up where he left off. The kingdom family was still the great longing of his heart. Fathers and sons, mothers and daughters, all living in the love of the Trinity. Times had changed but the longing of God had not. Zechariah was overwhelmed by Gabriel's words. At his age, he had long since given up hope of his wife, Elizabeth, and him being able to produce a son! As a result of his doubt, Gabriel told old Zechariah he would not be able to speak, until the prophecy came true.

Maybe Zechariah should have been aware the God of Israel had specialized in barrenness since the beginning of her story? But what if God wanted a trusted partner, like Zechariah, to experience a measure of the silence he himself had endured for 400 years? Either way, Zechariah's period of muteness provided him with a nine-month hiatus where he could meditate on the divine encounter he had received, allowing his heart and mind to expand in faith, preparing him to parent the boy who would 'make ready a people prepared for the Lord'. Not long after Zechariah's angelic visitation, his wife Elizabeth conceived and her weary heart was filled with an unspeakable joy.

Mary

Around the five-month mark of Elizabeth's pregnancy her teenage relative Mary also receives a visit from Gabriel. His words are dripping with heavenly favour: 'Do not be afraid, Mary; you have found favour with God. You will conceive and give birth to a son, and you are to call him Jesus.'

'How will this be,' Mary asks the angel with astonishing innocence, 'since I am a virgin?'[3]

Gabriel responds with some of the most poignant words in all of Scripture: 'The Holy Spirit will come on you, and the power of the Most High will overshadow you. So the holy one to be born will be called the Son of God.'[4]

Read that line again. The Holy Spirit will come upon (overshadow) you. Can you see what is happening? The Spirit is brooding again, only this time not over the watery chaos of creation but over Mary's womb. A seed of new creation is about to be planted by the Holy Spirit into the uterus of a teenage girl. The God who rules over the cosmos is about to take on the form of a single cell, submit himself to the process of cellular division and connect himself to a young virgin's womb via an umbilical cord.

Mary responds, 'May your word to me be fulfilled.'[5]

God has found a teenager he can trust, with his own life! Walking in the footsteps of her ancestors Abraham, Sarah, Moses, Hannah, Samuel and David, Mary yields her heart, her very body, to the plans and purposes of God in a posture of breathtaking availability. Mary's womb has become the ultimate holy of holies. God will be formed inside her. Mary will become the bearer of God's divine pleasure for all of humanity.

Joseph

Mary's fiancé, Joseph, does not receive the news well. His bride is pregnant. But not to him. Awkward. What would you think? Word of Mary's pregnancy, outside marriage, would have been viewed in Jewish-Torah circles as scandalous. The whole episode would be the talk of the town. To add insult to injury, the details of *how* she got pregnant make it particularly embarrassing. Mary has conceived by the Holy Spirit?! What in the world?! Surely this is all too much for the young Joseph to bear? The girl of his dreams has lost the plot. Despite his heart-break, the only thing Joseph can do to save his reputation is to divorce her. Technically Joseph has an exit route. According to the law he has all the permission he needs to get out of the relationship.

Remarkably, the Gospel of Matthew presents this young carpenter as embodying the true spirit of the Torah – kindness, mercy, love. Though there is no record of a single word spoken by Joseph, his actions speak louder than his words ever could. Matthew tells us Joseph is 'a righteous man'.[6] Imagine the internal dilemma going on in his sensitive heart. He loves Mary. Yet he has been deeply wounded. What is the loving thing to do? What is the right thing to do?

He decides to 'divorce her quietly' so she wouldn't be disgraced. He cares for her more than his own reputation. This is what righteous men do. God, however, is too committed to Joseph to let this happen. He wants Joseph to be the human dad of God's own Son. The Son of God will be born into a family unit, established on the union of a man and a woman, a reflection of the glory of the Eternal Family. But God knows Joseph needs some help to understand the crazy adventure he is being invited into. Graciously, God sends an angel to Joseph to inform him of the fuller story:

Joseph son of David, do not be afraid to take Mary home as your wife, because what is conceived in her is from the Holy Spirit. She will give birth to a son, and you are to give him the name Jesus, because he will save his people from their sins.

All this took place to fulfil what the Lord had said through the prophet: 'The virgin will conceive and give birth to a son, and they will call him Immanuel.'[7]

This is the divine assurance Joseph needs. When he wakes up, he begins to plan the wedding day. Joseph's reputation will be questioned, and a shotgun wedding is certainly not what he originally intended, yet his radical obedience and daring faith result in the joy of one day holding the Son of God in his arms and the privilege of naming him Jesus – the Saviour of the world. His baby boy will be God's way of saying to the world, Emmanuel – *I am with you.*

The birth

As we know by now, The God Story rivals any Hollywood blockbuster for drama. Yet there is nothing fictional about its narrative. The Scriptures tell the real flesh-and-blood history of our world. The world of Mary and Joseph was one defined by empires, slavery, pagan deities, oppressed people, war, revolutionary zeal and power. The emperor of the day was Caesar Augustus who had become the self-avowed saviour of the world, the one who claimed to have restored peace to the Roman Empire. As Mary and Joseph embarked on the challenging months of pregnancy, Caesar decided to hold a census of the people. A standard show of strength for any emperor: let's count how many people we own. This was the world where people are treated as commodities, mere numbers. Everyone in the province was commanded to go to their own town to register. For Joseph, being of the line of David, this meant a journey to Bethlehem, also known as David's City, with his *heavily* pregnant wife.

It's important to notice the deft touches of the Gospel authors. Skilfully, they build a portrait of the wider geopolitical context while at the same time focusing on where the real action is taking place. Caesar may be abiding in luxury, enjoying dominion and wealth, but for Matthew and Luke the indisputable focus of attention is a young couple making an arduous journey to Bethlehem.

Not long after Joseph and Mary made it to Bethlehem, labour kicked in. The census meant Bethlehem was heaving with people. Everywhere was booked up. Mary and Joseph couldn't get a room anywhere. A dirt floor at the front of a typically humble Judean dwelling – the place where animals were housed during the night – would have to do. Joseph made it as comfortable as possible for his young bride. Imagine him taking a deep breath and wiping sweat off his brow as he prepares himself to deliver the baby. Imagine Mary, pushing through agonizing contractions, experiencing pain beyond what she thought was bearable. As labour intensifies, Mary finally lets out one excruciating cry, pushing her baby into the world.

Joseph, wholly devoted, wraps the baby in swaddling clothes, lays him on Mary's breast and lies down beside his exhausted wife. Together they gaze upon their son, Jesus. Two hands. Two feet. A body. Two eyes. Two ears. A mouth and nose.

God will have a face like ours.

God, fully human in every way.

It's impossible to do justice to the mystery and magnitude of Jesus' birth. Yet we can appreciate something of its nature. That's the point, actually. For the God of the universe, the Almighty Creator, has come to us in a body we can see, touch and hear. The unseen ineffable Presence has become tangible, present to us, in our world, on our turf. The second Person of the Trinity has taken on flesh forever. From the moment of his conception Jesus will hold our humanity at the centre of the Eternal Family forever. Let's allow that holy mystery to sink in.

Word. Flesh. Dwell.

The apostle John who wrote the fourth Gospel begins his book differently from Matthew, Mark and Luke. John's introduction (the first

18 verses) is what Pete Greig describes as the 'punk-rock theology'[8] of its day. In these verses of punchy poetry John presents us with an ingeniously remixed version of the creation narrative itself. One succinct sentence in particular, found in verse 14, brings us right to the centre of The God Story, and contains layers we will unfold forever:

The Word became flesh and made his dwelling among us.[9]

The choice of words is precise and deliberate. Three distinctive words are used. **Word. Flesh. Dwell.** All these words are packed with rich themes we have highlighted through the narrative to date but which are now being woven together in the birth of Jesus.

Word (*logos*)

Logos was a word of real substance in John's day, both biblically and culturally. *Logos* can mean either 'reason' or 'word' (as in 'a spoken word'). Technically, it can actually mean both at once. This is *exactly* why John is using it. The intelligent minds of John's day were influenced heavily by Greek philosophical thought and they used *logos* to mean 'the big idea', the reason and wisdom behind all that exists. John's audacious claim that Jesus is the *Logos*, therefore, meant he was arguing that Jesus was the ultimate expression of reason. The intangible concept proposed by philosophers for centuries had now become a tangible reality. A person who could be touched, heard and seen. At the same time, John believed Jesus was the personification of God's spoken word (the other way of translating *logos*). Here, John was provoking his Jewish readers! God's spoken Word for the Jews was fundamental to their existence. Everything had come into being through God's Word. For Jews, God's spoken word was one with God's own character. John's claim was gloriously blasphemous. Jesus will be God's definitive word. When God wants to say something, it will look like Jesus.

Flesh (*sarx*)

Sarx is the word John uses to describe how God literally 'enfleshed' himself to humanity. The Greek *sarx* was then translated *caro* in

Latin, and it's from here we get the word 'incarnation'. The incarnation therefore literally means the 'enfleshment of God'. Jesus is God in the skin of a baby. The God who has reigned over the cosmos from the beginning, longing to fill it all with his presence, has chosen to limit himself to one language and location, confine himself to one culture and be raised in one family.

Dwell (skénoó)

Skénoó in the original Greek is a derivative of the same word used for 'tabernacle' or 'tent'. John's sentence therefore literally reads, 'The Word became flesh and tabernacled among us.' The localized 'hot-spot' of God's presence on the earth, fundamental to the plot to date, is no longer to be 'centred' on a tabernacle or a temple but a person: Jesus Christ. The intersection of heaven and earth is now an animal's feeding trough in a humble dwelling in Bethlehem.

'The Word (logos) became flesh (sarx) and made his dwelling (skénoó) among us.' Amen!

Angelic flash mob

On the face of it, the surroundings of this unprecedented event are pretty underwhelming. Yet contrast this with the dramatic activity going on in the heavenly realms. After 400 years of silence things have reached fever pitch. Uncouth shepherds serving on the night-shift are the first to get caught up in the angelic party.

Initially they are confronted by a lone angel: 'I bring you good news that will cause great joy for all the people. Today in the town of David a Saviour has been born to you; he is the Messiah, the Lord.'[10] This angel is suddenly joined by a multitude of heavenly hosts. Imagine the Judean night sky lit up by this vast angelic choir. A spectacular heavenly flash mob gathered solely for these plain-speaking, humble shepherds, declaring in unison:

Glory to God in the highest,
And on earth peace, goodwill toward men![11]

These refrains delivered by the angelic messengers are full of what we might call covenant promise language. In other words, they are a reformulation of those paradigm-shaping words spoken to Abram 2000 years before, 'I will bless you . . . and all peoples on earth will be blessed through you.' Something is happening in line with the ancient promises – the blessing of God for all nations is coming, joy for all people.

Just, no one expected it to happen the way it would.

Jesus' birth to 12 years old

When Jesus was only eight days old, in order to fulfil the customs of the Jewish law, he was taken to be circumcised. Jesus was not going to abandon Israel but fulfil Israel as *the true* Israelite. Some of the remnant, who had prayerfully and humbly held on to prophetic hope, longed to witness the ancient promises of a Messiah be fulfilled. Simeon, one of those devout ones who had waited in faithful expectation, got his reward.

Simeon felt a nudge to go to the temple on the day of Jesus' circumcision. He travelled the same route he had walked many times before. Only this day was different. Seeing the baby in the arms of Mary and Joseph, he knew something wonderful was taking place. Simeon gestured to Mary as if to say, 'Can I hold him?' As the old man took the newborn child in his arms, Luke records the overwhelming joy he experienced:

> With my own eyes I've seen your salvation;
>   it's now out in the open for everyone to see:
> A God-revealing light to the non-Jewish nations,
>   and of glory for your people Israel.[12]

Simeon, in this spontaneous, Spirit-inspired dedication moment, declared the universal hope tied up in the destiny of the newborn baby he was staring into the face of. Simeon would soon close his eyes for the last time but at that stage of his life he had never felt more whole. All his hopes and dreams had been realized in this baby boy.

The Gospel accounts do not give much more detail on Jesus' early life. We are left to imagine Jesus as a baby, having his nappy changed, nursing from his mother. It's fun to think of Jesus moving into the challenging toddler months, crawling around his dad's workshop and taking his first steps. Picture him learning how to speak. We can ponder what Joseph experienced the first time he heard Jesus say the word 'Abba' or what Mary felt the first time she heard Jesus pray. We know Mary and Joseph settled in the little Galilean town called Nazareth, so we can imagine Jesus growing up in a tight-knit community, sharing meals with neighbours, walking to the local synagogue with his family and playing tag with his friends.

The next account we have of Jesus' life is when he is 12 years old. Luke records him attending Jerusalem with his parents and siblings for Passover. As the festival comes to an end and many pilgrims begin the long journey back home, Jesus gets left behind in the capital city. It takes Mary and Joseph a day to discover he is missing, and three days to find him.

Luke's record of this event allows every parent to feel less guilty about their parenting skills! Imagine losing your teenager, who just so happens to be the Son of God, in a major metropolis for 72 hours! But Luke, a particularly astute writer, has other reasons for recording this episode. First of all he wants us to know it's *Passover* time. The Passover, as we have discovered, points back to a defining and unforgettable moment in Israel's history. Jesus is fully immersed in Israel's tradition and the theme of Passover will follow Jesus throughout his life.

The other significant detail Luke records here is Jesus' age – 12 years old. At this point in Jesus' life we can imagine him navigating all the awkwardness of puberty: his voice beginning to break, the first signs of facial hair appear and his need to manage his body odour! Yet Jesus would also be moving through a particularly unique rite of passage for young Jewish boys. This is the time when Jesus and his peers would be commissioned to take responsibility for their own development in the Torah. Parents, particularly the mother in Jewish culture up until puberty, nurtured their children in Israel's story and Scriptures. This threshold moment would be marked by an affirmative 'father's blessing'. For many Jewish boys, this was the point their apprenticeship to their father in the family business would begin. Jesus' incredulous response to his parents when they eventually find him in the temple courts debating the Scriptures therefore takes on a more profound depth of meaning:

Did you not know that I must be about My Father's business?[13]

Jesus' apprenticeship to Joseph in the carpentry shop is about to begin, but as we hear Jesus say 'my Father' for the first time, we become aware of an even greater apprenticeship under way. Jesus' young heart has begun to burn with love for his heavenly Father, and from this point on, 'Jesus grew in wisdom and stature, and in favour with God and man.'[14]

Growing up in Galilee

Remarkably, after this incident in Jesus' childhood we have next to no knowledge of what daily life was like for him. It's slightly puzzling to think Jesus had 33 years to save the planet and most of them weren't recorded! We are left with the question, *what was Jesus really like?* We can be sure he was a great friend, an honourable son and a caring big brother. We can safely presume he was a devout Jewish boy who prayed the Psalms and regularly attended the synagogue. But who were his best friends? What were his hobbies? What games did he play with his brothers and sisters? What piece of furniture did he enjoy making the most? Did he ever have romantic feelings?

We don't have answers, only playful imagination. What if these obscure years of Jesus' life are intentionally unrecorded to provoke a holy mystery about the everyday ordinary?

What if we are supposed to imagine Jesus simply rejoicing in the sheer delight of his Father, soaking in the 'very good' of creation, unhurried as he revels in the sacredness of his humanity? What if we are supposed to smile at the thought of Jesus laughing heartily with his friends, finding joy in the love of his family, purpose in the work of his hands, gratefulness in the produce of the land and deep contentment in his local community?

Isn't it reassuring to know Jesus wasn't a prolific child-evangelist or prophetic superstar?! Jesus didn't 'over-spiritualize' life. Jesus *lived* life. He tasted all the joys and sorrows each one of us experiences through life. He experienced the sheer delight of creation and felt acutely the full weight of the damage it has endured. Jesus knows what it is like to grow up with the stigma of an 'illegitimate birth', to be a refugee, to be poor, to lose a parent when you are young, to take on responsibility for your siblings, to earn a living from a hard day's work, to live in a 'backward' place which is despised by others, to experience loneliness, to be single your whole life. *Jesus knows what all that is like and more.* Jesus gets us. Those who grew up with Jesus struggled to accept his divinity, but many of us today struggle to accept his humanity. This is a great loss, for in Jesus God has associated with our humanity in a dramatic and intimate way.

As we reflect on Jesus' formative years we don't know for sure what he was doing at 15, 21 or 28 years of age. But we can be sure it involved ordaining the ordinary and filling the mundane with meaning. Jesus' unrecorded years remind us that every breath we take is a gift of grace and every place the soles of feet tread can be holy ground.

Cousin John, the baptizer

At 30 years of age, Jesus' days as a local carpenter began drawing to an end. Joseph had died at some point in Jesus' young life. Jesus knew the time was coming for him to step further into his destiny, yet many questions and memories swirled around his head and heart. What about his widowed mum? What about his young siblings? Imagine all the nostalgia Jesus experienced around his dad's business as he prepared to hang up his apron for the last time; the tools they had shared together, the smell of the wood, the products Joseph had taught him to make. Nevertheless, Jesus knew, like his great ancestor Abraham, the time had come to leave the comfort of home and start walking. Imagine a tear rolling down his cheek as he said goodbye to his mother, turning around to wave one last time as he walked further away from his childhood home.

The word on the street was the Spirit was moving in the desert through an unhinged prophet called John. All four Gospel writers reference the ministry of John the Baptist as fulfilling the ancient prophecies. He was the 'voice of one calling: "In the wilderness prepare the way for the LORD"';[15] the new Elijah,[16] the one who had come to turn the 'hearts of the parents to their children, and the hearts of the children to their parents'; the forerunner who would set the scene for the main event. Interestingly, John's way of doing this was not from the bright lights of the city but from the dusty edges of the desert lands of Judea. He was more prayer-room than platform, more of an idiosyncratic prophet than a polished orator. To add to his enigmatic nature, he wore clothes made of camel hair and lived off locusts and wild honey. Yet his message and his life were so radically captivating and powerful that Matthew tells us, 'People went out to him from Jerusalem and all Judea and the whole region of the Jordan.'[17] The intrigue with John, however, was less to do with his odd appearance and more to do with the potency of his message. It had been too long since the people had witnessed a true prophet in their midst.

John's words brought a bold and urgent challenge: Israel needed to wake up. Something was imminent. Like early morning sun rays which pierce the darkness before the orb of the sun is fully visible, John wanted the people to realize something was beginning to break into the world and everyone needed to pay attention. John's particular way of declaring the imminence of what (who) was coming was captured in the punchy refrain: 'Repent, for the kingdom of God is near.'

A great Light was about to shine. A new King was coming to establish God's reign on the earth. To pledge allegiance to this King required a dynamic reorienting of one's life. *Metanoia* is the Greek word for 'repentance' and its original meaning pointed to the act of turning around and walking in a whole new direction. John's words passionately challenged people to face the truth, and in doing so to turn their lives around. Although John's message was confronting, many were impacted by it. Crowds confessed their sins and were baptized by John in the River Jordan. A new way really was being prepared, hearts began to soften and the atmosphere started to shift.

As you might imagine, John was on a collision course with the authorities. Despite the words of the prophets of old declaring how faith in Yahweh should produce mercy, justice and humility, the religious system of the day had stopped producing such fruit. Further, many who held positions in the temple system exemplified the failure of the priesthood for many centuries. Rather than the humble stewardship of the presence of God, they were known for their love of money and power more than of God, using the temple for personal gain and status. It's fair to say John wasn't impressed:

> You brood of vipers! Who warned you to flee from the coming wrath? Produce fruit in keeping with repentance.[18]

This is dramatic language. God was moving and John the Baptist's listeners needed to prepare themselves. Yet John knew his role was only a dress rehearsal for the main event. He couldn't have been clearer on this:

> I'm baptizing you here in the river . . . The main character in this drama – compared to him I'm a mere stagehand – will ignite the kingdom life within you, a fire within you, the Holy Spirit within you, changing you from the inside out.[19]

John's deference to the 'main character' of the story is arguably the most incredible example of humility in all of Scripture. John would not be seduced by self-promotion or jealousy even when his own followers thought Jesus was stealing his limelight. He knew the limits of his calling began and ended in the role of 'best man'. He knew he was not the groom. His greatest joy was found in the elevation of his cousin, the One who had become his Lord: 'He must become greater; I must become less.'[20]

John will forever be the number one example of how to be number two. His life inspires and informs each of us towards a mature understanding of how we play our part in The God Story. Only as we lay down our own lives (decrease) do we fully embrace our role in the story and experience the deep joy of bringing glory (increase) to the main character.

Baptism in beloved

After months of preaching and proclaiming the imminence of the kingdom of God, one day *John sees Jesus!*

This is the moment John has been waiting for all his life. He has seen the One all of Israel has been waiting for. Incredibly, however, it seems no one else is caught up in the drama! Jesus, the humble carpenter from Nazareth, has followed the crowds into the wilderness and casually joined the back of the baptismal queue. Imagine Jesus, meekness personified, standing in the line of sinners. A stunning picture of his identification with humankind's brokenness and a signpost to how he will bear their judgement. John, preparing his latest preaching from the banks of the River Jordan, has lifted his head to gaze upon the throngs of people gathered that particular day. As he scans the crowd he locks eyes with Jesus. Imagine John's heart skipping a beat as holy adrenaline begins to flow through his body. In some supernaturally intuitive way God has made it clear to him that this One standing in the baptismal line is the Christ, the Chosen One, the Messiah.

As John, somewhat bewildered, tries to process his revelation, Jesus calmly waits his turn for baptism. Eventually Jesus enters the water and wades towards his older cousin. John thinks this could only happen one way: 'Surely you must baptize me, Jesus?' he argues. Imagine Jesus smiling at John, grabbing his arms enthusiastically and saying, 'Let's do this, John, now is the time. In order to fulfil all righteousness. You must baptize me.' John follows Jesus' instructions and lowers him into the River Jordan, the same river Joshua led the Israelites across 1500 years earlier. This time, though, it's not the waters that split open but the heavens. As Jesus comes up out of the water, divine delight pours forth as the Eternal Family dances over the River Jordan; a stunning expression of their loving union breaking out on the earth.[21]

The Spirit descends upon Jesus' drenched head in the form of a dove and the Father speaks the most tender, affectionate and desiring words ever uttered on the earth:

This is my beloved Son, with whom I am well pleased.[22]

There are so many other words the Father could say – more instructive words, more pragmatic, more strategic – *but he chooses these words*, words the Father has waited Jesus' whole life to declare over him publicly; *I love you and I'm pleased in you.*

But the thing is, Jesus hasn't really done any ministry at this stage. No miracles, no followers, no sermons; basically all the things Jesus is famous for. Why is this significant? The Father's words aren't based on achievement or earning. His words flow from a heart motivated by unconditional affection. Imagine how Jesus must feel these words deeply. The road ahead will be hard, a price will be paid no one can fathom. He will only be able to fulfil the mission that lies ahead of him through a deep awareness of the Father's belovedness. Abba's favoured words are the perfect culmination and summary of what the first 30 years have been all about: maturing in sonship.

Jesus would never forget these words.

Neither should we.

For as the Father ripped heaven open to announce his delight over Jesus, he was also declaring them over each one of us.

You are my beloved, I am well pleased in you.

In one sentence, humanity's two greatest struggles, fear-filled performance and shame-based rejection, are put to rest by the powerful belonging and approval of Abba Father. The eternal longing of his heart is to baptize you in belovedness. Hear his voice echo throughout the caverns of your soul.

You are my beloved, I am well pleased in you.

These are the words each of us was born to hear. Wherever we may be in the world, no matter how far we have run, these words go out from the heart of God to every son of Adam and every daughter of Eve.

Allow them to bring you home,
Beloved.

Presence: The Word has become flesh and dwelt among us. The hot-spot of God's presence, once the holy of holies in the tabernacle, has now become the body of Jesus. God has come close to us. Jesus is God with skin. God can be touched, heard, seen. Also Jesus shows us what a human being walking in intimate friendship with the Father looks like. Everything he does flows from a place of beloved sonship.

Family: The words of John the Baptist at the start of the New Testament pick up from the words of Malachi at the end of the Old Testament. A picture of unified generations is a sign that the way of Jesus is being prepared. God is making his home on the earth in the context of a human family. Jesus will have a mum and a dad and be nurtured and formed through the family structure he will be raised in. God is living in his own original design. As Jesus apprentices his father, Joseph, he is simultaneously learning the ways of his heavenly Father. After 30 years of maturing in sonship Jesus will hear words of divine pleasure from the Father: 'You are my beloved Son and I am well pleased with you.'

Kingdom: As the angels declare 'good news of great joy for all peoples' at the birth of Jesus we can hear the same covenantal language contained in God's promises to Abraham – blessing to all nations! In the 30 years Jesus spends enjoying the gift of everyday life and revelling in his Father's creation, we see the kind of kingdom God is bringing to earth. Everything Jesus touches is being made holy again, all of creation will be renewed.

Jesus, thank you for becoming like us; for identifying with us in the closest possible way; for showing us how to live a life of beloved sonship/daughterhood. Father, help us to hear your words 'You are my beloved' spoken over us. May we live from this place, enjoying the wonder of who you are and all you have made.

Questions for reflection: Encourage your heart to be still. Sink into God's presence and listen for the whisper of 'You are my beloved' spoken over you. In what parts of your everyday life might Jesus be wanting you to notice his presence?

8

The King

As Jesus walked out of the River Jordan everything changed:

> At once the Spirit sent him out into the wilderness, and he was
> in the wilderness forty days, being tempted by Satan. He was
> with the wild animals, and angels attended him.[1]

Jesus was led not to the bright lights of the city but to the inhospitable reality of the wilderness. Sometimes the Spirit's leading is not where we might expect it. The wilderness, as we have come to learn, however, is the painful gift which reveals where the true source of our identity is found. One might have thought Jesus' years in relative obscurity were over, but 40 days alone in the harshness of the wilderness lay ahead for him. The 30 patient years before had laid the deep foundation of identity. Now all of what had been formed in these years would be put to the test.

As Jesus fasted and prayed through 40 days, 'wild animals, and angels' surrounded him. This was a mixture of intense spiritual warfare and gruelling physical endurance, a test that would have pushed the most experienced adventurer to breaking point. Matthew, a master in understatement, says that at the end of these 40 days, 'he was hungry'![2] Imagine Jesus physically weak, mentally stretched and emotionally drained. Satan seized his moment. Three times Satan came to Jesus. His primary tactic hadn't changed. Deception. The grandmaster of identity theft we discovered in the Fall now launched the same attack upon Jesus he had on Adam and Eve.

But this time it didn't work. Ironically, while Jesus' body was weak, his spirit had never been stronger. Jesus may have been fasting but *he was also feasting* on the Father's words which had spoken right into the core of his being, 'you are my beloved Son in whom I am well pleased.'

Jesus was ready.

The first temptation

'If you are the Son of God, tell these stones to become bread.'[3] The first temptation was for Jesus to find *pleasure and provision* outside the presence of God. Jesus answered, 'It is written: "Man shall not live on bread alone, but on every word that comes from the mouth of God."'[4] Jesus wanted Satan to know he didn't need to self-provide. He was more than satisfied in the Father's words.

The second temptation

Satan came again, this time taking Jesus to the highest point in the temple, saying, 'If you are the Son of God . . . throw yourself down. For it is written: "He will command his angels concerning you, and they will lift you up in their hands."'[5] The second temptation was to strive for *prestige and performance* outside God's will for his life. Jesus' response to Satan this time was, 'It is also written: "Do not put the Lord your God to the test."'[6] This time Jesus reminded Satan that he didn't need to do something spectacular to prove himself; he trusted the Father's plan for his life.

The third temptation

As Jesus looked out over the world from a high mountain, Satan whispered, 'All this I will give you . . . if you will bow down and worship me.'[7] The final temptation was to seize *power and position* outside beloved sonship. Jesus responded, 'Away from me, Satan! For it is written: "Worship the Lord your God, and serve him only."'[8] Jesus' final rebuke was one of scorn! He wanted Satan to know he didn't need fame. Who the Father says he is is more than enough, and his worship and affection belong to God alone.

Pleasure and provision; prestige and performance; power and position – all of these are ways of finding identity outside the Father's love. Every time the enemy comes Jesus pushes him back with the word of God. Jesus will not be lured out of his beloved identity into the idolatry of self. Spiritual warfare, we learn, isn't a degree in demonology. It is the ability to stand in secure sonship.

The enemy left the wilderness with his tail between his legs. Jesus had been tempted in every way a human being can be, but as a new Adam and a *true* Israelite he stood his ground and resisted the demonic assault. He overcame where both Adam (in the garden) and Israel (in the wilderness) had failed.

The foretold serpent-crushing liberator promised from the Garden of Eden had come into the world as a confident, beloved Son.

The Nazareth manifesto

Jesus returned from the wilderness 'to Galilee in the power of the Spirit . . . He went to Nazareth, where he had been brought up'.[9]

Jesus came back home. Nazareth. On what appeared a typical Sabbath day, he attended the local synagogue. On this particular Saturday Jesus was handed the scroll to read, a routine occurrence in Jewish worship gatherings. But in a divinely synchronized turn of events Jesus 'just happened' to be given a passage from the prophet Isaiah. Slowly he read the following words to those who were present:

The Spirit of the Lord is on me,
    because he has anointed me
    to proclaim good news to the poor.
He has sent me to proclaim freedom for the prisoners
    and recovery of sight for the blind,
to set the oppressed free,
    to proclaim the year of the Lord's favour.[10]

Quietly Jesus rolled up the scroll, gave it back to the attendant and sat down. But something had happened. A holy suspense descended upon everyone gathered. 'The eyes of everyone in the synagogue were fastened on him.'[11]

Try to imagine the pregnant pause that gripped this little Nazareth synagogue. Jesus hadn't launched a bold new political campaign. He hadn't even raised his voice. Jesus simply recited words first uttered 700 years earlier, and as he did the whole atmosphere became charged with the manifest presence of God. Everyone could feel it.

God in the flesh had just read his own bio, the inaugural sermon of his coming kingdom. Granting the congregation a moment to process what had just happened, Jesus then gently but unapologetically confirmed what was happening:

Today this scripture is fulfilled in your hearing.[12]

Jesus' unveiling of his true identity may not have been a typical coronation moment in worldly terms. The synagogue in this little Galilean village was certainly no Lincoln Memorial or Westminster Abbey. Nonetheless, this was a crowning moment for Jesus. His style was calm and self-effacing but his claim was audacious. 'Today the scriptures are being fulfilled,' a modest way of saying, 'I am Israel's Messiah, the fulfilment of more than 300 prophecies from God's holy prophets, and I am bringing about the reign of God.'

Isaiah, the perfect speech-writer for such an occasion, had provided the words that would serve as Jesus' manifesto for the days ahead.

Good news was coming for the poor.

Freedom would come for the oppressed.

The blind would see.

Justice and liberation would be unleashed in all sorts of directions.

Everyone in that synagogue understood the magnitude of what Jesus was claiming. But tragically they couldn't accept it. Moments of revelation were stolen by overfamiliarity. '"Isn't this Joseph's son?" they asked.'[13] Picture the community murmuring among themselves, 'This is just the local carpenter!', 'Jesus?! He's just one of us.'

A pattern of misunderstanding and contradiction had begun. Jesus' glorious inaugural speech would end with his home-town community trying to throw him off a cliff!!

The anointed King

Before we move on from Nazareth it's crucial we understand the close connection between the words 'Spirit' and 'anointed' that Jesus had just recited over his own life.

> The Spirit of the Lord is on me, because he has anointed me . . .

Throughout the Old Testament the word 'anointing' was used in a number of different ways. One of the main ways was in connection with the visible sign of God's Spirit coming upon his people. Often when individuals were anointed they were simultaneously empowered by the Holy Spirit for the task that lay ahead of them. For example, when Samuel anointed Saul and David as king, on both occasions we are told the Spirit of God came upon them.[14] This particular association of the Spirit's anointing with Israel's kings is important as we bring it back to Jesus in Nazareth. The words of Isaiah 61 which Jesus quoted to launch his public ministry pointed to the fact that Yahweh's chosen servant would be clearly *anointed* by the Spirit of God.

Jesus wanted those who knew him best to realize all the prophetic themes of The God Story to date were coming together in his life. The dove that had come upon Jesus at his baptism had been a sign not just of divine favour but also of divine empowerment. *Jesus the Son* was now being marked out, through the Spirit's anointing, as *Jesus the King*. The word for anointing in Greek is *chrio*, the term from which we get Christ, or Messiah in Hebrew. 'Christ' therefore is not Jesus' last name but the title that marked him as the Spirit-filled Messiah who had come to bring about God's rule. Jesus is the anointed King, and from this point on he would do nothing outside the Spirit's infilling presence.

The kingdom of God

With Jesus' public ministry launched we enter into the main substance of each of the Gospel writers' accounts: Jesus' kingdom
mission. One reason these authors spend so much of their Gospels
focusing on Jesus' three years of ministry is because this theme of
kingship in Israel's story was so strong. As we learned in Chapter
4 at a crucial hinge-point in The God Story, Israel under Samuel's
leadership had rejected the Lordship of Yahweh. They wanted a
human king like the other nations. God had agonizingly granted
their request but it was never Plan A. God had warned these kings
would become self-serving and lovers of power, and for many years
Israel had borne the consequences of this decision. The reign of
their kings looked nothing like the loving justice and righteousness
of Yahweh.

Against this backdrop, the Gospels present Jesus announcing
the re-establishing of God's reign on the earth. Plan A was being
reinstated. The world was about to be flipped right side up again,
turned on an axis of self-giving love, and Jesus called this new
reality 'the kingdom of God'. It was Jesus' favourite thing to talk
about.

Defined simply, the kingdom of God is the place where God is
acknowledged as King; where God's will and God's ways are realized. Or another way to put it is, the kingdom of God will always
look like King Jesus.

Imagine if God's will and God's way were to become the reality
in our world. What if Jesus were king of every motivation of your
heart, every meditation of your mind, every decision in your day,
every relationship you form? What if Jesus were king of your work
day and your off day, of your eating and your entertainment, of
your money and your sexuality, of your education and your social
media? If Jesus were king in all of your life and your family's lives,
what might this look like?

Then broaden your imagination to think about what it would
look like if Jesus were king of your neighbourhood; what if Jesus
were king of every sphere of influence in your city – education,

business, health, media? And what would it look like if God's will and God's ways were a reality over the nations? Jesus came to turn these 'what ifs' into a present reality. To see God's desires for creation fulfilled.

We must read on in the Gospels to see exactly how Jesus did this. But first we must take note of Jesus' method for bringing about the kingdom of God. As the second Person of the Trinity, what Jesus had always enjoyed in heaven he would now reproduce on the earth.

Family.

The kingdom family

The early focus of Jesus' mission was to intentionally establish a circle of friends. He invited men and women to literally leave everything and follow him. Jesus' hope was twofold. First, Jesus wanted them to become like him. This is what being a disciple was all about. Jesus would give his disciples a 'backstage pass' to all aspects of his life so they could emulate him *in all of life*. He didn't want 'water-carriers' to help him get the work done. Jesus wanted friends he could draw into the fellowship of his heart. The disciples were never victims of Jesus' vision. Rather they were central to his vision.

Second, Jesus wanted to form a new family on the earth, nothing less than the Eternal Family's dream from the beginning: a holy community participating in the establishment of God's will and God's ways throughout the earth.

Jesus' choice of friends wasn't exactly eye-catching, though. Initially Jesus chose 12 men, a clear sign of how the family he was gathering to himself was a fulfilment of Israel's 12 tribes. But on the face of it these guys were pretty ordinary at best! Further, recruiting them together in a team seemed like a recipe for disaster.

Imagine your core team was made up of the sweet-spirited Nathaniel and the deceitful Judas. What about a Roman-compromised tax collector called Matthew sharing the same room when out on mission with a Jewish Zealot called Simon? How does that even work? And then there were the two sets of brothers, all 'blue-collar' fishermen – the earnest Andrew and his full-throttle brother Peter teamed up with the competitive James and John whom Jesus had nicknamed 'The Sons of Thunder'. One moment James and John asked Jesus if they could call fire down on a Samaritan village and in another they got their mum to ask Jesus if they could have the most privileged places in heaven. Realistically, this team shouldn't have worked. Different political opinions, different backgrounds, different expectations of Messiah, all swirling together in the midst of power-hungry testosterone and out-of-control egos.

Add into this the fact that Jesus deliberately made space in this team for women,[15] despite the cultural taboos associated with such. We can only imagine the gossip and slander Jesus' team was the subject of. And yet the establishment of this circle of thoroughly underwhelming candidates would become Jesus' way of revealing to the world what God's kingdom really looks like. The disciples would observe Jesus and participate with Jesus; they would be empowered by Jesus and rebuked by Jesus; they would believe Jesus and doubt Jesus. They would defend Jesus and even deny Jesus.

But in the end they would learn to love like Jesus. They would learn to love one another more than themselves. They would learn how to be the family of God.

The kingdom announced

Accompanied by his new followers, Jesus left Nazareth and began announcing the kingdom of God in the surrounding towns and villages of Galilee. Jesus' plain-speaking and succinct way of proclaiming the kingdom was, 'Repent, for the kingdom of God has come near.'[16] By saying 'come near', Jesus was not claiming that the kingdom of God was new, but rather that an astonishing new level of accessibility to God's will and God's ways had come. Through Jesus' own physical body, God's loving and just rule was coming upon the earth in an unprecedented way. 'Reach out and touch it,' Jesus was saying.

Announcing the kingdom of God gave Jesus great joy. He said to his hearers, 'it gives your Father great happiness to give you the Kingdom.'[17] Imagine the Father smiling as Jesus went around announcing the kingdom. No wonder Jesus called it 'good news', another way of saying 'gospel'. The kingdom was 'good news' because Jesus had come to reveal the love of the Father and to destroy the works of darkness. The kingdom was 'good news' because a glorious reversal of the Fall was taking place. Bodies would become whole and hearts would be set free; wrongs would be made right and the downtrodden would be lifted up; marriages would be restored and enemies would be reconciled; poverty would be alleviated and the lonely would be welcomed in family. Everything humanity was powerless to conquer, Jesus had come to defeat; and everything humanity was truly longing for, Jesus had come to complete.

The way to enter into this kingdom was clear. *Repentance.*

Jesus had built upon the theme his cousin John had laid the foundations for. Only an act of 'giving yourself up' and turning your whole life around (*metanoia*) would position you to receive this kingdom. This is why 'good news' and 'repentance' are connected. A glorious new beginning happens when we repent.

The term 'good news' derives from the Greek word *euangelion*, mostly used in military circumstances to announce the victory of a new king. Imagine a royal subject running into a village after a battle, heralding the 'good news' of his king's victory. Within this context Jesus' 'good news' naturally challenged people's allegiance to other kingdoms. Jesus was calling people not only to repent from sinful behaviour but also to relinquish their allegiance to opposing kingdoms to enable them to embrace the rule of his kingdom.

Jesus' kingdom announcement was set into a swirling hurricane of opposing kingdoms. On the one hand, Rome's empire ideology swirled around most of Europe and the Mediterranean. The Emperor Caesar Augustus had claimed to be 'the son of God', ordering inscriptions and monuments to be carved all over the Empire promoting his self-acclaimed divine rule. Augustus claimed to have brought peace, justice, security and prosperity to the world. On the other hand, aggressive waves of Jewish nationalism were gathering force. Most Jews carried fervent aspirations of liberation and deliverance from Rome. They believed as the chosen people of the One Creator God, despite the setback of exile, that a mighty deliverance in the form of a Davidic, warrior-type king had been promised. Jesus' call to repentance carried the serious challenge to relinquish trust in these alternative ways to establish peace, justice and prosperity in the world. Every misplaced hope for humanity's ultimate flourishing must be replaced in Jesus. 'Seek first the kingdom of God'[18] was an invitation to come follow him, steep ourselves in a new God-reality and participate with him – the *true* King – in his loving reign.

The kingdom described

Jesus was both a preacher and a teacher! He announced the kingdom of God but also took time to describe it. What did God's will and ways on the earth actually look like?

Through the use of parables, stories and conversations sometimes delivered in the synagogues but often shared around tables and on boats, Jesus articulated the culture of the kingdom of God. His words carried a dimension of wisdom his hearers had never heard before. 'No one ever spoke the way this man does,'[19] they remarked. As Robert Jenson says, 'he interpreted the scriptures as if he had written them. He interpreted them in a way that really only the author might be entitled to interpret them.'[20]

This teaching genius of Jesus was characterized by a theological dexterity that matched the most prolific of rabbis grounded in word-pictures and streetwise language that were easily understood. His words were full of 'Spirit and life,'[21] captivating followers from every stratum of society. His accessible metaphors of water, bread, seeds, children, business and money naturally hooked his hearers' attention. He drew them into another world and all the possibilities of deeper and more meaningful life in the kingdom of God.

That, of course, doesn't mean that what Jesus said was always easy to hear. His use of stories and parables often shook people out of their current erroneous worldviews, rattling their religious cages and challenging the narrow-mindedness of their thinking.

Jesus' description of the kingdom of God is best captured by Matthew in what we now call 'The Sermon on the Mount'. Matthew framed Jesus' teaching as the fulfilment of Israel's story. Jesus was a new and better Moses. Jesus had overcome the wilderness temptations (Matthew 4), and he would now deliver *a new law* on *another mountain* for *a new humanity* (Matthew 5—9).

The opening section of The Sermon on the Mount is known as *The Beatitudes*. In eight pithy and punchy statements Jesus described the kinds of people who are being welcomed into the kingdom family. 'Blessed' is the anchoring word Jesus uses:

Blessed are the poor in spirit,
    for theirs is the kingdom of heaven.
Blessed are those who mourn,
    for they will be comforted.
Blessed are the meek,
    for they will inherit the earth.
Blessed are those who hunger and thirst for righteousness,
    for they will be filled.
Blessed are the merciful,
    for they will be shown mercy.
Blessed are the pure in heart,
    for they will see God.
Blessed are the peacemakers,
    for they will be called children of God.
Blessed are those who are persecuted because of
    righteousness,
    for theirs is the kingdom of heaven.

Blessed are you when people insult you, persecute you and falsely say all kinds of evil against you because of me. Rejoice and be glad, because great is your reward in heaven, for in the same way they persecuted the prophets who were before you.[22]

To all of those Jesus identifies, he says, 'Congratulations! You are the recipients of good news – welcome home, yours is the kingdom.' The Beatitudes are not to be understood as a list of entry requirements, addressed to a bunch of isolated individuals. Rather they are revolutionary hope-filled words declaring the 'good news' that those who have formerly felt 'outside' the kingdom of God are actually the ones best positioned to receive it.

From this mountain Jesus would go on to describe how he was not just welcoming this unlikely mix of people into his family but he was also forming them with his disciples into an alternative community. His inspired words laid out a vision for nothing less than a new human society. Revolutionary themes populated Jesus' words: enemy-love, radical self-denial and a whole new dimension of inner purity. But, perhaps most revolutionary of all, Jesus would teach his followers how to approach Yahweh as 'Abba, Father'. An intimate communion with the Father is what would characterize those who would become part of the kingdom family.

As radical as The Sermon on The Mount seemed, Jesus' words were entirely consistent with the Torah. He elevated its central features with fresh life-giving revelation and luminosity: 'Do not think that I have come to abolish the Law or the Prophets; I have not come to abolish them but to fulfil them.'[23]

Jesus was not replacing Mosaic tradition or the words of the prophets. He was fully revealing the perfect embodiment of them. As you might expect, though, Jesus' application of Torah flatly contradicted many of the standard interpretations of Torah the Jewish religious leaders had enforced on the people. Jesus rebuked them. His invitation to the crowds of listeners was clear: *Do you want the failed righteousness of the Pharisees or do you want the abundant life of Yahweh I am revealing to you?*

The Pharisees did not like being exposed. On one particular occasion, recorded in Matthew 22, they conspired together to try to denounce Jesus as a flaky interpreter of Torah, teeing up an expert in the Torah to catch Jesus out:

One of them, an expert in the law, tested him with this question: 'Teacher, which is the greatest commandment in the Law?'[24]

Before we get to Jesus' answer, some context is important. At this point in Israel's history, the Torah was summarized into 613 rules made up of 248 commands and 365 prohibitions. Some argue these rules were bolstered by as many as 1500 amendments. That's a lot of rule keeping, requiring an exhausting level of interpretative analysis. Jewish rabbis debated their varied applications of Torah, which led to the establishment of different rabbinical schools. In this scene, the Torah expert's agenda was to categorize Jesus as just one more standard rabbi holding his own interpretation of Torah – to corner Jesus on a technicality. As Jesus began his response, everything, it seemed, was going to plan for the Pharisees. Jesus quoted Deuteronomy 6.5:

Jesus replied: '"Love the Lord your God with all your heart and with all your soul and with all your mind." This is the first and greatest commandment.'[25]

These revered words declaring the Lordship of Yahweh over creation were recited in prayer every day by any faithful Jew. 'This is the first and greatest commandment,' Jesus said. Those listening would have expected nothing less. But then Jesus did something profound. Before the Pharisees could probe Jesus further, he continued:

And the second is like it:

What? What could possibly be 'like' the first and greatest commandment? Quoting another verse from the Torah, this time Leviticus 19.18, Jesus finished his sentence:

Love your neighbour as yourself.[26]

Taking this verse buried in the middle of the Torah – Leviticus 19.18 – and weaving it alongside Deuteronomy 6.4–5, Jesus performed the ultimate theological judo move ever played. The Pharisees' attempts to push Jesus into a theological submission move had only resulted in elevating the genius of Jesus' grasp of Torah. Jesus doubled down further. 'All the Law and the Prophets hang on these two commandments.'[27] Are you getting this? Jesus took all the Old Testament, all 613 rules plus all the Hebraic prophetic tradition, and summed it up in two commandments.

Love God.

Love your neighbour.

It is impossible to overstate how revolutionary this moment was for those listening. Jesus left no room for any more speculative theology – the goal of Torah and the central moral category of his kingdom was sacrificial love. *Vertical love* (love for God) is inseparable from *horizontal love* (love for one's fellow human being). This reinterpretation of Torah would lead to a reordering of the whole world. The kingdom of God is against everything that hinders love.

The kingdom demonstrated

Everything Jesus said he lived. The rightful king had landed on planet Earth. Heaven and earth had overlapped in a new way and *the effects were tangible*. Jesus was not just announcing and describing the kingdom; he was also demonstrating it. Everywhere Jesus went, he extended the jurisdiction of the kingdom of God. Each manifestation of heaven on the earth was a momentary taste of what the new creation to come would look like forever. Bodies, minds, hearts, bones, creation itself came into alignment with God's original design. These signs, wonders and miracles all testified to the power of the Spirit flowing through Jesus' body to broken humanity. Jesus was a zero-resistance home for the Holy Spirit, the happiest place the Holy Spirit ever lived. Jesus demonstrated how God's power flowing through a human being could change the world.

Ezekiel's river which had flowed away from the temple towards the Dead Sea was being fulfilled. Walking in the fullness of the Spirit, Jesus moved towards a humanity that had been broken by sin, unleashing freedom and redemption in all directions. Israel had lost a vision of who God really was, twisting and manipulating the Torah to define holiness as a negative, excluding force.[28] Jesus, releasing the Holy Spirit over the broken and dead places of humanity, revealed true holiness is a positive contagion able to conquer sin and administer the Father's life-giving, healing, transformative power wherever it flows.

All of Jesus' supernatural demonstrations of the kingdom were an expression of his Father's heart. Jesus had confirmed to his curious disciples that when they had seen him they had seen the Father.[29] No wonder every miracle was motivated by mercy. For Jesus' zeal to renew and restore individuals was an embodied expression of the tender heart of the Father for his broken but beloved creation. Everyone's story mattered to Jesus because each life was precious to the Father. We read of Jesus touching a leprous outcast, restoring his skin, and stopping the crowds to acknowledge a woman who had in her desperation for healing reached out to touch him. We discover him bringing a 12-year-old girl back to life in front of her grief-stricken parents and delivering a boy tormented by an evil spirit after hearing the heart-cry of a troubled father. Jesus gave dignity back to people: healing a man with a withered hand, giving sight to a blind beggar, multiplying a young lad's lunch to feed thousands and simply making space to value a Samaritan woman who had been used and abused for years.

To describe all of Jesus' demonstrations of the kingdom would take us well beyond the word limit of our book! But we are consoled by the apostle John who summarized his Gospel with the words, 'Jesus did many other things as well. If every one of them were written down, I suppose that even the whole world would not have room for the books that would be written.'[30] We will have to settle for a short overview of four main ways Jesus demonstrated the kingdom of God: healing, deliverance, forgiveness and celebration.

Healing

Moved with compassion, Jesus' healing virtue flowed into bodies riddled with sickness and pain, groaning under the tyranny of sin. 'Great crowds came to him, bringing the lame, the blind, the crippled, the mute and many others, and laid them at his feet; and he healed them.'[31] Every miraculous 'sign' of healing was a 'signpost' towards a vision of God's reign where sickness is conquered and death is defeated.

Deliverance

Jesus launched a full-frontal assault on the oppressive lies the enemy had bound people up in for far too long. Dark, oppressive spirits causing agonizing torment in the minds of the ones Jesus loved were driven out by the liberating light of his words, releasing them into glorious freedom and perfect peace.

Forgiveness

No matter where individuals had been, no matter what they had done and no matter what others said they deserved, Jesus welcomed people home to unconditional love. The kingdom of God was a condemnation-free zone. Weary souls, weighed down by a lifetime of guilt, offence and relational pain, were released into the intoxicating freedom of God's forgiveness.

Celebration

Jesus' demonstration of the kingdom also came in his joyful reception of every individual he encountered. Those labelled worthless by the world were seen and celebrated. Jesus sat at their tables to help them know they had a place at his. He developed a reputation for partying as much as he prayed because he was unashamed to confirm heaven rejoices over those who have been passed by.

Recounting all these ways Jesus demonstrated the kingdom stirs our heart to worship him. For when we have seen Jesus, we have seen the Father.

Kingdom and a cross

The truth is, everyone wants a king like Jesus.

But for the crowds listening to Jesus, it was so difficult for them to accept just how different Jesus' expression of kingship was. Even the disciples who were mesmerized by everything Jesus did and said were often perplexed. Jesus was just so different from any worldview they had of a king and so outside any of the main categories of Messiah the Jews had developed over the previous few centuries. It appears, even after a substantial amount of time with Jesus, they were still making their minds up about him.

A key moment in this process came as they arrived in Caesarea Philippi for another day of mission with Jesus. Imagine Jesus cutting through the chattering small talk with a provoking question, 'Who do people say that I am?' Now imagine a nervous tension begin to fill up the space around Jesus and his disciples. What was the right answer? How should they respond? Jesus had asked the question in the third person – 'Who do people say that I am?', which meant they had some wiggle room. At least they could answer on behalf of others. It wasn't personal. Yet. Picture the disciples responding, 'Well ... uh ... you know ... em ... some say you are John the Baptist ... and eh, some say Elijah or ahem [nervous cough, clearing throat] some say Jeremiah ... at the very least they definitely think you are one of the prophets.'

Silence. Awkward silence.

Then comes another question. The most important and penetrating question every human being could ever be asked.

Who do you say that I am?

The tension increases. Jesus has just moved the conversation from the edges of philosophical musing (*Who do people say that I am?*) to the most central of all existential questions (*Who do you say that I am?*). Remember, these disciples have witnessed Jesus heal the sick, raise the dead and calm the storm. They have been captivated by Jesus but haven't yet confessed Jesus as Lord and Messiah. It is that big a deal.

Peter *finally* breaks the silence:

You are the Messiah, the Son of the living God.[32]

The hairs on the back of the rest of the disciples' necks straighten and their hearts skip an extra beat. The air is thick with revelation. Peter's declaration, right in line with the Father's words at Jesus' baptism, has pulled the reality of heaven into earth. All the covenant promises and prophetic hopes of 2000 years are consummated in Peter's outburst. Jesus the Son, a carpenter from Nazareth, is the Christ. He is God's anointed King, the Messiah, the Lord of All.[33]

Jesus responds to Peter, 'Blessed are you, Simon son of Jonah, for this was not revealed to you by flesh and blood, but by my Father in heaven.'[34] Peter's role will be significant. From this time on Jesus will nickname him 'the Rock' but *it is the revelation – 'Jesus is Lord' – Peter has received*, not Peter himself, that will be the ultimate bedrock upon which Jesus will build his church. All those who declare and proclaim with their lives 'Jesus is Lord' will join Peter in the kingdom community. They will be granted 'keys of the kingdom' – free access into the Father's love and a Spirit-empowered authority to declare and demonstrate the kingdom of God on the earth. Peter has shown us the words of God in our mouths can be as powerful as the words of God in his mouth.

Imagine Peter swelling with pride after this 'top of the class' moment, dreaming of ruling alongside Jesus on a throne. Yet in this moment – the first time Jesus has been declared 'the Christ', the anointed King, by one of his followers – Jesus introduces an ironic twist. He pivots the focus of his journey towards a radically different type of throne. Incomprehensibly for the disciples, Jesus goes as far as to say that he is going to die and then be raised on the third day. No one has ever really thought the prophetic words about a coming deliverer would be combined with others about a suffering servant.[35] It is all too much for the disciples, especially Peter who, emboldened by his previous moment of glory, now gets it horribly wrong: 'Never, Lord! . . . This shall never happen to you!' he says before Jesus rebukes him, 'Get behind me, Satan! You are a stumbling block to me; you do not have in mind the concerns of God, but merely human concerns.'[36]

The rock on which Jesus will build his church has just become a stumbling block to God's eternal purpose. Talk about being

Presence: Jesus came proclaiming a whole new level of accessibility to the presence of God – heaven and earth were overlapping and interlocking in the body of Jesus. As Jesus made friends with people from every type of background he was vividly revealing God's desire to come close to us. Jesus' own life demonstrated the priority of the presence of God, withdrawing often to be with the Father and teaching his disciples to do the same – to abide in God's presence and to address God intimately as 'Abba'.

Family: Jesus' strategy for his kingdom mission was family. What he had always enjoyed in heaven he would now reproduce on the earth. Jesus built a team of friends around him who walked with him throughout his three-year ministry. He loved his own biological family but was welcoming everyone as his brothers and sisters. This deeply relational context was the place where Jesus discipled his friends. In the Sermon on the Mount Jesus revealed God's vision for nothing less than a new human society, a family established on sacrificial love.

Kingdom: Plan A was being reinstated. Jesus had come to restore God's loving rule and reign on the earth. As the Anointed One (the Christ), Jesus lived zero-resistant to the Holy Spirit's power flowing through his life. His life-giving words, prolific teaching and miracles were all signs revealing who the true King of the universe really was. The kingdom will always look like the King. Jesus had come to reorder the world on an axis of sacrificial love. The way to enter this kingdom was repentance – giving up every other allegiance and following Jesus and his kingdom.

Lord Jesus, thank you for coming to reveal to us the Father. For demonstrating what a life of abiding in the Father will look like – welcoming sinners, offering forgiveness, healing diseases, delivering the oppressed, celebrating the outcasts. We repent of every other love and allegiance, Jesus. We want to be your disciples.

Questions for reflection: Jesus revealed the heart of the Father! Why is it so crucial we understand this? At the heart of Jesus' ministry was his commitment to discipling those closest to him. Who are the people God has called you to disciple? Who is discipling you? Jesus lived with 'zero resistance' to the Holy Spirit. How can you grow in friendship and surrender to the Holy Spirit? Where do you long to see more of God's Kingdom 'on earth as it is in heaven'?

9

The Passion

Thirty years of ordinary life and relative obscurity.

Three years unveiling the kingdom of God.

And now, seven days that changed history.

If you knew you had only seven days left to live, what would you do? What would you want to say? Whom would you want to be with?

Here we stand in wonder, for The God Story allows us to peer intently into the activities of Jesus' final week. All four Gospels dedicate at least one-third of their books to these last days of Jesus' life. They had to. It was just that significant.

In Latin, the root of the word 'passion' means 'to suffer'. If you are familiar with the life and death of Jesus it will make sense why these concluding sections of the Gospels have become known as 'The Passion'. In truth, as the poet John Donne beautifully said of Jesus, 'all his life was a continual passion'.[1] But the final chapters of the Gospels reveal the degree of suffering God will endure to have what he passionately loves. At this crescendo moment in human history, divine desire and longing love, which have carried The God Story forward from the beginning, will be fully exposed in the most vivid and shocking of ways. As we move through the Passion Week, the rich tapestry of themes we have discovered throughout the biblical narrative are knit together dramatically in Jesus' actions.

Every day is a sermon in itself. Every action is deliberate and prophetic.

On Sunday a king

Jesus began his final week by making his way into Jerusalem on the first Sunday of Passover. Thousands of pilgrims had returned to Jerusalem to celebrate the great feast. Jesus had humbly begun the march to his enthronement riding on a little donkey as the crowds shouted 'Hosanna', meaning 'God saves.' This entrance evoked the ancient prophecy of Zechariah: 'Rejoice greatly, Daughter Zion! Shout, Daughter Jerusalem! See, your king comes to you, righteous and victorious, lowly and riding on a donkey.'[2] The imagery is both provocative to Israelite prophetic consciousness and subversive to Roman imperial rule. This act was the fulfilment of prophecy *and* the reframing of power. The people cheered but the Pharisees raged. And those who got closest to Jesus could see tears flowing down his cheeks as he wept over a city and a generation who would ultimately turn their backs on him.

On Monday a priest

The next day, Jesus, burning with zeal, strode right into the heart of the religious establishment. The Jerusalem temple had become a hive of corruption, idolatry, exploitation and greed. The poor, the maimed and the Gentiles had been granted only limited access to the temple courts. Enough was enough. Jesus began driving out the money-lenders, flipping over the tables of the animal-sacrifice dealers and rebuking the temple leaders with the words of the prophet Isaiah, '"My house will be called a house of prayer," but you are making it "a den of robbers".'[3] More than just tables were being turned upside down. A new priest had come to reveal that he was the true intersection of heaven and earth who would take us all into the holy of holies. Ultimately Jesus was the living temple – the eternal place of forgiveness, radical inclusion, healing justice and loving mercy for all peoples. This is what the house of God should look like.

On Tuesday a prophet

On Tuesday, as might be expected, Jesus had to deal with the fallout of his previous day's actions at the temple. But when challenged by the religious elite, Jesus did not back down. Jesus reminded the current generation that they were living in the stiff-necked legacy of their forefathers who rejected the Word of God. He likened them to the tenants of a landowner's vineyard.[4] A landowner who had sent his servants at harvest-time to return with some of the fruit. One by one the tenants had killed the servants. Finally, the land-owner thought they would respect his son if he sent him. But the result was the same. Driven by self-serving greed they killed him too. Israel had always killed its prophets and they would do the same with the greatest of them all.

On Wednesday a lover

On the relative calm of Wednesday a beautiful interruption took place as Jesus reclined with his friends at one of his favourite places: Lazarus' house in Bethany. Without warning, an unnamed woman carrying an alabaster jar entered the room and began to anoint Jesus, pouring expensive oil over his head. Imagine this oil smearing his face, soaking his clothes and staining the ground around him, the sweetest of fragrances replacing the room's arid smell. This costly, spontaneous act of worship had broken heaven open over the room. Those present were indignant at the reckless nature of the woman's deed. For the disciple Judas this was the final straw. But for Jesus this was a beautiful waste. She had ministered to the weary apprehension weighing upon him in this final week. 'She has done a beautiful thing to me,'[5] Jesus said, deeply touched by this woman's love. The sweet aroma of this woman's perfume would remain on Jesus' body for the rest of his life, and the testimony of her worship throughout all time.

On Thursday a friend

On Thursday, Jesus made preparations for a dinner with his disciples. It was time for the Passover meal and Jesus had longed to share this intimate space with those closest to his heart: 'I have eagerly desired to eat this Passover with you.'[6] As the disciples took their places around the table, Jesus, in an act of jaw-dropping humility, took off his robe, lifted a basin of water and a towel and began to wash his friends' feet. The disciples were visibly uncomfortable – a rabbi washing his disciples' feet? Peter objected. Jesus, not for the first time, corrected him. Peter had to learn the only way to enter the kingdom was to realize that Jesus needed to do something for him he could not do for himself. Jesus' foot-washing act was the perfect foretaste of what the next 24 hours would be all about – Jesus revealing his glory as the Servant King. Love to the uttermost.

In this atmosphere of breathtaking vulnerability the scene was set for Jesus to reveal more of the deep treasures of his heart to his friends.[7] The mood was thick with the kind of intense intimacy and heartfelt trust one experiences after years of seasoned and tested friendship. As they gathered around the Passover table, Jesus began to unfold the holy mysteries at the heart of the Eternal Family. Beautifully, he revealed how a way was being made for each of us to be caught up in the love shared between the Father, Son and Holy Spirit. Notice the intimacy of the Father and Son's relationship in the following words:

We [the Father and I] will come to them and make our home with them.[8]

I have called you friends, for everything that I learned from my Father I have made known to you.[9]

I am the true vine, and my Father is the gardener . . . I am the vine; you are the branches. . . Now remain in my love.[10]

Jesus wanted to prepare the disciples. He was going to leave soon, but he promised that he would not leave them as orphans. Further, he made the astonishing declaration that there was something better coming. The third Person of the Trinity was going to come – *the Paraclete*[11] – a Helper and Comforter, who would inhabit their whole beings in a new way. In some mysterious way, through the Spirit, Jesus and the Father would make their home in the human heart.

Caught up in the revelation of these intimate moments with his friends, Jesus began to pray. Meditating on the glory of the Father's love for him before the foundation of the world,[12] Jesus prayed out the dream of the Eternal Family from the beginning:

> I have given them the glory that you gave me, that they may be one as we are one – I in them and you in me – so that they may be brought to complete unity. Then the world will know that you sent me and have loved them even as you have loved me.[13]

Jesus then lifted some bread, gave thanks and broke it. Looking into the eyes of his disciples he said, 'This is my body given for you; do this in remembrance of me.'[14] He then lifted a cup. Gazing at each of his friends he declared, 'This cup is the new covenant in my blood, which is poured out for you.'[15]

Imagine what it was like for these young Jewish men to hear the words:

This bread is my body.

This cup is my blood.

The revolutionary nature of this centuries-old Passover meal moment cannot be overstated as the entire meaning of the meal was redefined. Jesus was the spotless Lamb who would become the perfect sacrifice for sin forever, the ultimate fulfilment of God's covenantal promises with his people. Bewildered, the disciples wouldn't have known what to say in this holy suspending moment. Jesus had the perfect solution. Worship. Jesus lifted his song to the Father and the disciples joined in.

Wouldn't you have loved to have heard that song?

Another garden

At some point the singing stopped. The intimacy of a table shifted to the loneliness of a moonlit garden, as Jesus walked out of the room into the dark of night. The warm scene of Jesus sharing the Passover meal with his closest friends was replaced with Jesus alone in a garden, suffering unthinkable torment.

Think of the vulnerability. A single 33-year-old man, carrying the collective weight of sinful humanity on his shoulders. His three friends whom he wanted to be with him had fallen asleep. Jesus, reaching out to them for help, had never felt more alone.

Think of the torment. Like vultures circling around their prey, every destructive and violent demon had been unleashed on Jesus at this moment. The enemy who had failed to seduce him in the wilderness came again. This garden was called 'Gethsemane', which means 'Olive Press'. In the same way olives would have been crushed in this garden, by heavy stones to squeeze out the oil, the merciless anguish Jesus suffered in Gethsemane caused the capillaries in his forehead to burst. Blood began to trickle down Jesus' face. In loud groans Jesus prayed out, 'My soul is overwhelmed with sorrow to the point of death.'[16]

Think of the temptation to wilt. At this point more than any other Jesus was acutely aware of the lure of 'self'. He cried out, 'Is there any other way, Father?' Jesus knew he could choose not to go through with the plan. As the Son of God he could call down legions of heaven's armies for help. But he also knew there was only one way The God Story could be fulfilled. He would have to go through what lay ahead as a human being.

It all hinged on his choice.

'Not what I will, but what you will.'[17] Three times Jesus, exasperated but wholly surrendered, would cry out the most courageous prayer ever uttered.

Adam and Eve had disobeyed in a garden of Eden, bringing a curse on all humanity. Jesus in the garden of Gethsemane chose obedience, liberating all of creation. Throughout history, humanity had been lured into the mastery of their own fate; 'Not your will,

God, but mine be done' had been the sound echoing throughout the world since Eden. Cain. Babel. Egypt. Babylon. Tragically, even Israel! But now one of Adam's sons had overcome temptation when all of hell was hounding him. Jesus chose to hand his destiny over to God, whatever that might mean.

'Not my will but yours be done.'

A great 'bruising' lay ahead, beyond what human minds can imagine, but the prophesied serpent-crusher had begun to crush the enemy's head. Because Jesus overcame the luring power of self, a way was being opened for you to overcome too.

At this moment a torch-bearing troop appears – an accompaniment of temple guards, Jewish leaders and Roman auxiliaries led by Judas. One of Jesus' disciples has blown his cover to the chief priests who, ironically, are now working in tandem with the Romans for Jesus' arrest. Jesus is betrayed by the kiss of one of his own. As the guards seize Jesus, all the disciples flee the scene. Jesus alone is dragged into the city to stand before his accusers: the Jewish Sanhedrin.

Peter follows at a distance but, standing with others around a fire in the temple courts, he is recognized as one of Jesus' friends. He denies he knows Jesus. Three times. A cock crows. Crushed, Peter realizes he has done the thing he said he would never do.

We've all been there.

On Friday the Lamb

Jesus' interrogation before the Jewish leaders endured through Thursday night and was followed by a Roman one, early Friday morning. Jesus was passed between the Roman governor Pilate and Herod – the so-called 'King of the Jews' – neither of whom was able to condemn Jesus for any breach of law. Pilate alone was left to make the call. He was reluctant to sentence Jesus, offering the crowd a deal. Setting Jesus against Barabbas, who had been imprisoned for murder, Pilate promised to release a prisoner. Barabbas or Jesus? He presumed the crowd would choose Jesus. Incredibly, the crowd, now caught up in a demonic frenzy, cried,

'Give us Barabbas.' Hoping a severe flogging would be sufficient for the Jewish leaders, Pilate gave his soldiers permission to perform the standard treatment criminals of the empire would suffer. Jesus was taken to the Roman fortress and ruthlessly whipped 39 times, mocked, punched and jeered at. To add to their perverse comedy, the soldiers savagely pressed a crown of thorns on his head. Brought back to Pilate, the now disfigured Jesus was presented before the people. Hoping this would be enough for them, 'Here is the man!'[18] Pilate declared. Unmoved by the savage brutality Jesus had already endured, the crowds cried, 'Crucify! Crucify!'[19] Pilate by this stage had been warned by his wife to have nothing to do with Jesus as she had been greatly troubled in a dream about him. But how could Pilate get out of this without losing face? The fear of God had gripped him but the fear of man was driving him. Addressing the crowds, Pilate tried one more time, declaring, 'Here is your king.'[20] The response from the Jewish scribes is astonishing.

'We have no king but Caesar.'

The elite at the heart of Israel's religious system had preached of a coming king who would vindicate Israel. But now their cover was blown. *We have no king but Caesar.* Seriously? Claiming allegiance to a pagan king even as the Word of God stood before them exposed what they were all about: self-seeking acclaim, reputation, power at the expense of others.

Pilate ultimately played to the crowd. He literally washed his hands of the whole affair and submitted to the shouts of the mob.

'Crucify him, Crucify him.'

Imagine Jesus standing alone in these moments. The Son of God experiencing the sound of cruel rejection as his own beloved creation called for his death.

Jesus was unjustly condemned for rebellion against Rome. The sentence was Rome's form of capital punishment. Death by crucifixion.

A cross-beam is laid across Jesus' flagellated back. He is ordered to carry it to a hill outside the city walls, called Calvary, a place also known as 'The Skull' (Golgotha). Here Jesus is stripped naked and stretched out on the cross he has just carried. Jesus does not fight back – like a little lamb entering the slaughterhouse. The soldiers drive pegs through Jesus' hands and feet and, as they do, Jesus' strained voice can be heard praying words that apply to every image-bearing human.

'Father, forgive them, for they do not know what they are doing.'[21]

Jesus is a king who would rather forgive his enemies than kill them.

As the cross is hoisted up and dropped violently into a hole in the ground, excruciating pain shoots through Jesus' being. Every part of his body convulses in agony.

Jesus is crucified between two thieves. One of the thieves begins to mock Jesus while the other springs to his defence. Despite Jesus' disfigured and tortured state, this thief can see the beauty of God hanging beside him. He cries out, 'Jesus, remember me when you come into your kingdom.' Despite his own agony, Jesus looks at his dying companion and says, 'Today you will be with me in Paradise.'[22] This criminal will soon close his eyes, drawing the curtains on a life filled with brokenness, sin and regret. Yet when he next opens his eyes he will only see Jesus in glory.

This is the gospel. It is never too late to say 'yes' to Jesus.

Some women followed Jesus to the cross, one of whom is Jesus' mother, Mary. John stands with these women beneath the body of his crucified Lord. Looking lovingly at his mother and his closest friend, Jesus speaks from the cross, 'Woman, behold your son; son, behold your mother.' From that day on John will take Mary into his own home.

This is the kingdom family.

At noon, darkness falls for three hours. Creation responds in fear and trembling as the curse of sin, deep in the very fabric of the earth, is dealt with. Hanging on the cross, Jesus endures the darkest hours in human history as a perfect, sinless substitute for all humankind. God in his mercy has allowed himself, the judge of all, to be placed under his own sentence. Through the willing offering of Jesus, God came in the Son to save humanity from the just penalty of sin and to set right what was wrong. Jesus took our place, allowing the sins of the world – past, present and future – to be absorbed into his own body. Identifying with us at the extremities of our fallenness, Jesus *became* sin for us.[23]

Bearing such an unimaginable weight of sin and enduring unfathomable levels of physical pain, Jesus cries out, 'My God, my God, why have you forsaken me?'[24]

There is no reply.

Silence.

Horrible, nebulous, resounding silence.

This is without doubt the most inconceivable moment in The God Story. The Son, who had always enjoyed unbroken union with God, was now experiencing in his full humanity the agony of *forsakenness*. Jesus was inhabiting the chasm sin created between us and the Father. It's really hard to wrap our minds around the mystery of these moments, but ultimately this is not a theological conundrum to solve. It is an incomprehensible love to enter into. What we can say is *Jesus was not alone*. The Father, the Son and the Spirit endured these extreme moments of desolation together for our sakes. The Father was not operating over and against Jesus on the cross but through and in Jesus, upholding him on the cross by the power of the Spirit.[25]

'All this is from God, who reconciled us to himself through Christ . . . God was reconciling the world to himself in Christ.'[26]

In the life and death of Jesus, the triune God identified with us at the deepest possible level. Jesus' moments of 'forsakenness' on the cross now emphatically confirm what The God Story has shown us at numerous points already: the Maker of the Universe is a co-suffering God. God, in Jesus, not only entered into our pain, our loneliness, our dysfunction, our 'hell' but also experienced it; he took our pain into his own body.

'Surely he has borne our griefs and carried our sorrows.'[27]

Breaking the harrowing silence of these moments, Jesus cried out from the cross, 'I am thirsty.'[28] Jesus may have been physically parched but this thirsting spoke to something deeper. This was his identification with the aching cry of the human spirit for the only thing that can satisfy it: the unfailing love of the Father.

In the final moments of Jesus' life he would end his ministry just like he started it. In perfect submission he entrusted his life to the Father.

'Father, into your hands I commit my Spirit.'[29] Having already quoted the first verse of Psalm 22 on the cross – the cry of forsakenness – now, in his final moments, Jesus' prayer of surrendered trust in the Father is an echo of the rest of Psalm 22 where the writer declares his confidence in God's continued presence despite great suffering.

But before Jesus breathed his last breath, he had one more thing to say. One more truth he must *proclaim*. It may not have been the loudest cry in history, given Jesus' agony, but it was the most powerful. And nothing would stop him from proclaiming it. Gathering up every ounce of energy left in his punctured body, Jesus lifted up a cry.

'*Tetelestai.*'

It is finished.

Nothing would ever be the same again. A revolution had begun. Buildings shook, rocks split in two, graves opened, principalities and powers were destabilized as 'it is finished' rang out from Golgotha.

The most powerful of these signs was a supernatural tearing of the temple veil – the curtain that protected people from God's holy presence on the earth. The veil was torn from top to bottom. As Jesus cried out from the cross, imagine the Father's own hands extending down through the heavens to earth and ripping the veil in two. Jesus had allowed his own body to be broken apart for the sins of all humanity because God couldn't stand the distance. The temple curtains could now be ripped open to welcome everyone into the presence of God. No longer would the presence of God be restricted to one person, in a physical building, only to be accessed once a year. Now the presence of God was on the loose, moving beyond the building into all the dislocated, forgotten and fractured parts of the world, pursuing lost sons and daughters in relentless love.

The paradox of the cross

The cross was and is the ultimate of all paradoxes. As Jesus hangs on the cross we are exposed to the worst of humanity and the best of God. The darkest hour of history became the place that revealed the brightest light that ever shone. In those hours when the sun refused to shine, humanity reached its lowest – killing the Lord of glory in the barbaric act of crucifixion. Evil had thrown everything it had at Jesus, but his willing sacrifice meant that ultimately evil had been drained of its power. In the most self-sacrificial act in history, we find the most powerful redemptive act in history.

Hans Urs von Balthasar powerfully concludes, 'Being disguised under the disfigurement of an ugly crucifixion and death, Christ upon the cross is paradoxically the clearest revelation of who God is.'[30]

God has progressively unfolded himself in covenant vulner-ability to the point where he has not only taken on flesh but he has allowed himself to be lifted up, naked and bleeding, on a cross. Now there is no longer any question who God is – pierced and crushed, God is Love!

On Saturday a grave

Jesus' followers could see none of this at this point, though. All they knew was Jesus was dead. Jesus was laid in a tomb, and the devastating emotional trauma of Friday shifted into the hollow and horrible stone-cold reality of Saturday. The day when Love endured the silence and mystery of unanswered questions and broken dreams.

On Saturday, everything hurts like hell.

The first day of a new creation

Most of the world was still sleeping when the greatest miracle in history surreptitiously began to take place. Something unique and unprecedented was happening in the very soul of creation and no one even knew it was happening. As the first specks of light punched through the darkness of Saturday night, awakening creation to another Sunday, the birdsong was different. The orb of the sun slowly pushed its way above the Earth's horizon, accompanied in the skies by a chirping chorus of delight, the trees of the field clapped their hands and the seas resounded with praise. A cacophony of joy was welcoming hope's eternal spring. This was the first day of a new creation.

Heartbroken Mary

Mary Magdalene, completely bereft of the man who had loved her like no other man ever had, went to Jesus' tomb before most people were awake. As she lay awake in the dark of Friday night, tears streamed down the sides of her face and collected in her ears. The only thing that would help in this grief-stricken moment was to be close to the body of the one she had loved. But Saturday was the Sabbath. Jews couldn't be near the dead on the Sabbath. Sunday morning was her earliest opportunity to get close to Jesus' body.

As she arrived at the tomb, desperate to be near her Lord, she was not met by Roman soldiers keeping guard over the tomb but by a man dressed in white. Her bewilderment was compounded by the fact that the stone which had been blocking the tomb's entrance was rolled away. As she stood, overwhelmed with confusion and fearing Jesus' body had been stolen, the man in white spoke to her:

> Do not be afraid, for I know that you are looking for Jesus, who was crucified. He is not here; he has risen, just as he said. Come and see the place where he lay. Then go quickly and tell his disciples: 'He has risen from the dead and is going ahead of you into Galilee. There you will see him.' Now I have told you.[31]

Bewildered, Mary ran to tell the disciples, her heart pounding in her chest, her mind racing with questions. What would the others think? Was this really true? Had her lack of sleep caused an apparition?

On hearing the news, Peter and John rushed to the tomb, only to confirm what Mary had declared. Jesus was not there! But where was he? Peter and John returned to their hideout to process what was happening. Mary remained by the tomb, alone. Overwhelmed and retraumatized by the absence of Jesus' body, she began to weep. Looking into the tomb one more time, she saw two angels seated where Jesus' body had lain. When they saw her tears they asked her, 'Woman, why are you crying?'

'They have taken my Lord away,' Mary cried out through her tears, 'and I don't know where they have put him.'[32]

At this point Mary heard the gentle probing question again, 'Woman, why are you crying?', only this time from a different source. As she turned to see whom she assumed was the gardener, a second question followed, 'Who is it you are looking for?'

Resurrection comes asking us questions.

Why are you crying?

Who are you looking for?

Mary pleaded desperately, 'Sir, if you have carried him away, tell me where you have put him, and I will get him.'[33]

And then he said her name:

'Mary.'

Imagine the beauty of this moment. Into the midst of Mary's utter hopelessness she hears her king, the Lover of her soul, say her name again.

'Mary.'

No one says our name like Jesus does. Imagine the familiar cadence of Jesus' voice reverberating lovingly through every cavern of Mary's soul, awakening everything that has died within her. And now all she wants to do is to hold him.

All the Gospel writers want us to know that the core gospel message – *Jesus has risen from the dead* – was entrusted to a woman. A woman who had been defined by brokenness, torment and abuse – before she met Jesus – had become the herald of new creation. Mary's declaration to the disciples – 'I have seen the Lord' – turns the pages of The God Story into a whole new chapter.

From this point on a great redemptive reversal will shape the unfolding narrative.

Disillusioned disciples

Everything that had happened over the previous few days had left the disciples confused and disorientated. They were also fearful of the Jewish leaders, so they shut themselves up in a house. What would their association with Jesus mean for them now? Later that night Jesus appeared to them. We aren't sure how Jesus got into the locked house; we are only told, 'Jesus came and stood among them.'[34]

Standing before his astonished friends, bearing the marks of his death in his resurrected body, Jesus simply spoke the word 'Peace'. The God Story does not describe Jesus 'explaining' the resurrection to the disciples. His presence is enough.

'Peace.'

It was all going to be OK. 'Resurrection means the last thing is never the final thing.'[35]

Doubting Thomas

Thomas had missed Jesus' appearance to the other disciples. Afterwards, when they told him what had happened, his response was cynical.

'Unless I see the nail marks in his hands and put my finger where the nails were, and put my hand into his side, I will not believe.'[36]

Thomas needed to see for himself. He may have doubted, but equally he wasn't prepared to live off someone else's testimony.

Jesus, unintimidated by his doubts and questions, wanted Thomas to have his own encounter. Eight days later, Jesus came to the same house, speaking 'peace' again to his disciples. This time, though, Jesus addressed Thomas directly, gently inviting him: 'Put your finger here; see my hands. Reach out your hand and put it into my side. Stop doubting and believe.'[37]

Awed and humbled in this moment, Thomas realized he didn't need to reach for Jesus' hands and feet. For as the resurrected Jesus stood before him, he had never been more certain Jesus had reached out to him. Knowing this was more than enough.

With heartfelt words of renewed faith Thomas could only say, 'My Lord and my God!'[38]

Defeated Peter

Peter returned to fishing. Jesus had risen from the dead but the regret of his betrayal lingered. Peter hadn't forgiven himself. So he decided to go back to what was familiar. Fishing. But this wasn't going well either. John records how they had a bad night on the lake and caught nothing. The empty boat mirrored the emptiness of Peter's soul.

In the distance Peter could see the outline of a man instructing them to throw their nets on the other side. Staring at empty nets and realizing they had nothing to lose, they did as he said. An enormous amount of fish were hauled in. Recognizing it was Jesus who had called to them, Peter jumped out of the boat, wading quickly through the water as the other disciples pulled the nets ashore. Jesus had a fire ready and invited them to bring their catch to the breakfast BBQ. As Peter sat around the burning coals, the smoky aroma took his mind back to the fire he had stood around a few weeks before, the fire of betrayal. While the others joked with Jesus over breakfast, Peter felt distance between him and Jesus as he relived the shame over again. But for Jesus, the fire was exactly what Peter's soul needed. Sometimes the way to a man's heart is some food and a fire to stare into!

As they finished eating, imagine Jesus looking across the fire and asking Peter a question. 'Peter, do you love me?'

Resurrection comes asking questions.

Peter replied quickly: 'Yes, Lord,' he said, 'you know that I love you.' In reply Jesus said, 'Feed my lambs.' But then Jesus asked Peter again, 'Peter, do you love me?' Picture Peter a little bit uncomfortable now, wondering where Jesus was going with this line of questioning. Peter replied again, 'Yes, Lord, you know that I love you.' Again, the same instruction from Jesus: 'Take care of my sheep.' Imagine the awkwardness spreading among the other disciples, pervading the atmosphere around the fire. And then the question came a third time. 'Peter, do you love me?' Initially,

Peter was hurt and humbled. *Why did Jesus ask me this in front of the others three times?* And then it dawned on him. For every time Peter had denied Jesus in front of others, he had been given an opportunity to declare his love for Jesus in front of others. Shame would not be allowed to outscore love. The guilt Peter had carried for days began to dissolve within him. This was Peter's recommissioning. Jesus had never lost a vision for Peter's destiny and this was the moment to remind him of it. Peter was still the one on whom Jesus would build his church. Only now Peter was even more qualified. He had blown it and now he had been restored. Forgiven by grace and rebirthed in resurrection hope, Peter had experienced the gospel. He was the perfect candidate to lay foundations in the kingdom family.

The resurrected Jesus comes asking us questions – deeply personal questions.

Why are you weeping?

Who are you looking for?

Do you love me?

These intimate encounters speak powerfully to our own souls. Like Mary, Thomas, Peter and the disciples, who witnessed the scars in Jesus' resurrected body, we can now recognize there is no dark or broken place we can get to that Jesus has not already been to on our behalf! He has been to hell and back for us and he has come back victorious. Now we know nothing can separate us from his love, for the Passion of God could not be held in the tomb. Love is stronger than death.[39]

Heartbroken Mary would love again. Doubting Thomas would believe again. The disillusioned disciples, full of fear and confusion, would have peace again. Defeated Peter would be restored in love and recommissioned to live with courage again.

As wonderful as Jesus' restoration of each of these disciples was, he was still not finished with them. All of these broken-made-beautiful friends of Jesus would be entrusted with the full weight of his authority to carry out God's dream in the world. Along with others, they would hear Jesus' empowering words before he left them:

All authority in heaven and on earth has been given to me. Therefore go and make disciples of all nations, baptizing them in the name of the Father and of the Son and of the Holy Spirit, and teaching them to obey everything I have commanded you. And surely I am with you always, to the very end of the age.[40]

Jesus' resurrection had ushered in all kinds of new possibilities.

A whole new creation was just beginning.

And the ones Jesus loved would be at the forefront of it.

Presence: The cross of Christ leaves us in no doubt, God could not stand the distance between himself and humanity. Jesus willingly offered himself up to free us from sin so we might come into the full knowledge of his presence in our lives. Jesus' death ripped open the temple veil. No longer would the manifest presence of God be restricted to one person, in a physical building, only to be accessed once a year. Now the presence of God was moving into all the broken parts of the world, pursuing us in relentless love.

Family: Jesus carried his family and friends with him right through to the end. He cried out to the Father the night before he died that his followers would know the same love the Eternal Family enjoyed. Jesus longed to be with the Father but equally longed for the disciples to share in this loving union. It would be their love for one another that would define them as his disciples. They would learn to wash one another's feet. Even as Jesus hung on the cross, looking at his mother and John, he was thinking of the kingdom family.

Kingdom: As Jesus cried it was 'finished', the power of every rival kingdom was defeated. As he rose from the grave, new creation had begun. The glorious everlasting kingdom of the future was ushered into our present reality. Jesus had revealed the kingdom for his three years of ministry on the earth. Now through his death and resurrection he was handing the keys of the kingdom on to his followers. They would carry his authority into the world, embodying Jesus' love and power in their own lives.

Father, no words can express our gratitude for the cross. Jesus, thank you for dying for us, for freeing us from our sin, for bringing us into a living relationship with you. Thank you that we can live in your love, find a home in your family and walk into a glorious future. We praise you for rising triumphantly from the grave, defeating sin, death and hell. You are our risen King!

Questions for reflection: How does the suffering love of Jesus meet the places of pain and suffering in your life and story? How does it make you feel to know Jesus died to bring you into the glorious presence of the Eternal Family? How empowering is it to think that the same Spirit which raised Jesus from the dead now lives in us?

10
The Church

The greatest movement the world has ever known started with the most absurd command.

'Wait.'

How do you start anything by doing, well . . . nothing?!

Jesus knew that if the disciples were going to go and change the world, the last thing they needed to be relying on was their own adrenaline. They had just spent three years with God-in-the-flesh experiencing every emotion possible; in recent days they had watched the Son of God conquer death and appear to them throughout 40 days as the risen Lord. It would be understandable that they might think nothing could stop them now. But relying on their own strength would be a disaster:

Wait . . . you will receive power when the Holy Spirit comes on you; and you will be my witnesses in Jerusalem, and in all Judea and Samaria, and to the ends of the earth.[1]

The disciples needed to get off on the right foot. Everything from this moment on would be a gracious act of God through the gift of the Holy Spirit. The Spirit's coming was 'the promise of the Father' – the way divine desire and longing love would pulse throughout the earth after Jesus returned to heaven. Jesus had started a movement. The third Person of the Trinity, God's own intimate breath, would now carry it forward.

After Jesus said these words he ascended to heaven. A cloud took him up from their sight. Imagine the disciples looking into the sky as everything Jesus had prepared them for became a stone-cold reality. Had Jesus really left them in charge? Two angels broke the mood of bewilderment. 'Why do you stand here looking into the sky?'[2] These men dressed in white described how Jesus would come again just like he had left. It was time to get on with things. Well, not quite.

'Wait,' Jesus had instructed.

Pentecost

Ten days after Jesus ascended to heaven, the disciples were still waiting – 120 of them. Lingering together in a room, reassuring one another of the words of Jesus.

'Suddenly a sound like the blowing of a violent wind came from heaven and filled the whole house where they were sitting.'[3] The same wind which had created beauty out of nothing at the beginning of The God Story, the same wind which had blown over the Red Sea to bring about a great deliverance for the Hebrew slaves, was now blowing through a room in Jerusalem filling human flesh with the eternal breath of God.

'They saw what seemed to be tongues of fire that separated and came to rest on each of them.'[4] The same fire Moses watched burning through a bush, the same fire the children of Israel watched light up the sky above Mount Sinai many years before, was now igniting the hearts of men and women, brandishing them in flames of holy love.

'All of them were filled with the Holy Spirit and began to speak in other tongues as the Spirit enabled them.'[5]

The room the disciples were gathered in had been completely broken open by a sovereign move of God. A great prophecy of old had been activated and men and women were undone by the power of the Holy Spirit. God was doing what he had always promised to do: pouring himself out on humankind, bursting from within them.

Pentecost was always part of the plan. Another great Jewish feast was now being fulfilled. The vivid symbolism of wind and fire we have identified as manifestations of God's presence throughout the Old Testament confirmed something new was happening.

God's centrepiece plan for humanity, the dream of the Eternal Family, was beginning to be unveiled. Through the coming of the Spirit humankind would be completely inhabited and immersed with God's breath, carrying the presence of Jesus to the ends of the earth. Simply put, Pentecost was the moment the Holy Spirit birthed what we now call the Church.

Wind and width

The wind of the Spirit that came upon those gathered in the upper room turned them inside out. They would never be the same again. The power latent in the breath of God *moved* them from the place they had settled and it would keep moving them for the rest of their lives. Like sailboats blown into uncharted waters, the furious longing of God would propel these early disciples into places they had never imagined they would go. It thrust them onto the streets of Jerusalem, declaring the good news of Jesus, *in new languages.* Thousands of Jewish pilgrims, who had returned to Jerusalem to celebrate Pentecost, began hearing these Galilean men and women speaking in the *mother-tongues* of the regions they had travelled from. 'Each of us hears them in our native language,'[6] the startled crowds declared, hearing the intimate language of the Father. The power of the Pentecost wind had given the disciples the gift of communicating God's longing love, beyond the understanding of their minds. As Willie Jennings says, Pentecost confirms that 'God speaks people, fluently.'[7]

The supernatural nature of this event needed some definition, however. The ecstasy needed explanation. A leader was needed.

'Peter stood up with the Eleven.'[8] Courage stood tall. This was Peter's moment. He cleared his throat and opened his mouth. As Peter started speaking, the language of heaven poured forth from his lips. The Spirit was on him.

Peter preached the gospel with authority. He wove the words of the prophet Joel with his own, teaching how this particular Pentecost was central not just to Israel's destiny but also to the whole world. This is what God had been preparing his people for through the prophets but which the majority of Israelites had missed. 'Fellow Jews', Peter cried out, 'this is what was spoken by the prophet Joel:

> In the last days, God says,
>   I will pour out my Spirit on all people.
> Your sons and daughters will prophesy,
>   your young men will see visions,
>   your old men will dream dreams.
> Even on my servants, both men and women,
>   I will pour out my Spirit in those days,
>   and they will prophesy.[9]

Peter's bold declaration was this: the life, death, resurrection and ascension of Jesus had defined history. Now this 'last days' promise of the Spirit had been activated. Jesus had been the pioneer citizen of a new humanity, revealing what a Spirit-filled life looked like. His obedience to the Father had now made it possible for all humanity to be filled with the Spirit.

Remember, Jesus had tried to prepare his disciples for this before his crucifixion: 'But I am telling you the truth: it is better for you that I go away, because if I do not go, the Helper will not come to you.'[10] What could have been better than God in the flesh?

The only answer – God in *all* flesh!

Imagine – God wants to make his home inside ordinary people like us. All of us!

Israel had crucified the Messiah, the Son of David. Yet the astonishing good news shaking up Jerusalem was, 'it was impossible for death to keep its hold on him.'[11] Jesus had risen. Forgiveness of sins was now available to all, even to those who had cried 'crucify him' a few weeks earlier.

The authority and anointing resting on Peter's words broke through the deception and hard-hearted tradition of many of those gathered. Many of the hearers, 'cut to the heart', responded, 'what shall we do?'[12]

Peter replied, 'Repent and be baptized, every one of you, in the name of Jesus Christ for the forgiveness of your sins. And you will receive the gift of the Holy Spirit. The promise is for you and your children and for all who are far off.'[13]

Three thousand people accepted the message that day and were added to the disciples. *Three thousand!!* How would the disciples know what to do with this amount of people turning to Jesus in a single day? The disciples did exactly what Jesus did with them.

Form them into family.

Fire and depth

The fire of the Spirit that rested on the early disciples not only set their tongues on fire but it also ignited a white-hot flame of passion in their hearts. This fiery baptism would deeply form the disciples, burning up everything in them that was opposed to love. This love overflowed from their lives, forging the disciples of Jesus together into a family.

The Greek word for this depth of connection the early church enjoyed together is *koinonia* – a much richer word than our English translation 'fellowship'. *Koinonia* speaks of a sacred bond, a circle of belonging fostered through a common and shared cause.

The *centrifugal effect* of the Spirit which had propelled the disciples outward to proclaim Jesus was matched by a simultaneous *centripetal force* binding each new believer *into* this new community. All who received the 'good news' were welcomed extravagantly into the kingdom family and former strangers were knit together by the Spirit.

Sacrifice was the fuel that caused the early church to burn bright with love for Jesus. But it wasn't any easier for them than it is for us. Nevertheless, the Holy Spirit had flooded their lives with the love of Jesus. Any sacrifice was a cost worth paying.

It's no wonder, then, that this fledgling kingdom community was marked by devotion – a combination of *sacrificial love* and *wholehearted commitment*. The first house churches in Jerusalem we read of in Acts 2.42–47 expressed this devotion in regular practices of prayer, the breaking of bread, studying the teachings of Jesus and generous hospitality.

Their radical commitment to the way of Jesus and the evidence of his power through miraculous signs and wonders were the main causes of the early church's exponential growth. God was alive among this beautiful community. It's no wonder people were added to their number every day. The description of this first Jesus-community helps us develop a simple thesis for how we understand the Church: a prayerful family on mission surrendered to the Holy Spirit.

Jerusalem and Judea

Acts will go on to tell the story of a people so broken open by the Spirit that they would go to places their feet had never gone (width) to form families with people they previously had never known (depth), or wanted to know!

Luke provides the thrilling account of how a small, persecuted Jerusalem sect would emerge and multiply to become a worldwide phenomenon. His description follows a certain plot structure shaped on the final words of Jesus, 'you will be my witnesses in Jerusalem, and in all Judea and Samaria, and to the ends of the earth.' There are days we wish Luke told us more, like what happened to each of the disciples from this point? Where did they get to with the gospel? How did they die? But what Luke does tell us, though, in a masterful account, is the story of how the gospel of the kingdom would be preached and embodied in Jerusalem and then to all nations.

As the wind of the Spirit blew upon these early converts in Jerusalem, what emerged was an unstoppable grassroots movement, led not by the educated and elite but by ordinary women and men who had encountered the Spirit of the risen Lord.

New converts were formed in Christlikeness in the new Jesus-communities emerging all across Jerusalem. These small house churches embodied the countercultural nature of the kingdom of God and became a powerful witness to the watching world. They became known as places where rich and poor gathered together to sing songs, pray and celebrate the meal Jesus had left them with. They were identified as communities who served the needs of the poor and destitute, welcoming the orphans, unwanted babies and widows right into the middle of their fellowship. When sickness hit these densely populated cities and many fled to escape disease, the Jesus-followers were known as those who stayed to look after the sick and dying.

The spontaneous nature of this movement of ordinary, everyday believers was held in beautiful harmony with the influence of the apostles.[14] These 'unlearned' men, whom Jesus had discipled in the ways of his kingdom, had stepped into a destiny beyond their wildest dreams. Measured against the power and prestige of Rome, these men would have been viewed as insignificant nobodies, and within Jewish rabbinical circles they had been overlooked. Yet through the anointing of the Spirit the disciples of Jesus became leaders of this new movement spreading across Judea. Peter and John's healing of a lame man at the temple in these early parts of Luke's account confirms how their lack of worldly credentials was exactly what made them so powerful. All they had was Jesus, and this was more than enough:

> Silver or gold I do not have, but what I do have I give you. In the name of Jesus Christ of Nazareth, walk.[15]

These miraculous signs and breakthrough moments which often characterized the apostles' lives were key for the expansion of the kingdom. But it was the way the apostles embodied the servant-hearted nature of Jesus, demonstrating an ability to establish these new kingdom communities on the right foundations, that ensured the flourishing of the early church movement. As well as the original 12, a number of other men and women emerged to carry this apostolic grace.

First of all Stephen would enter the narrative as a leader of one of the first churches planted in Jerusalem. We initially meet him as one of seven Spirit-filled waiters, serving food to widows. Stephen was viewed by the religious establishment as a threat to the status quo. They were right to view him as such because he was carrying the power of a different story. When questioned by the authorities Stephen boldly preached The God Story. Like Peter at Pentecost,

Stephen declared how Israel's story had been fulfilled in Jesus of Nazareth, whom the Jews had crucified. His accusers didn't like it. Israel's leaders dealt with this word from God the way they always had. Another prophet was murdered.[16] His accusers stoned him but, as the stones pummelled against his body, Stephen, now joined to Jesus, was able to cry, 'Lord, do not hold this sin against them.'

Stephen's death sparked a wave of persecution towards the early Jesus-followers. The persecution resulted in a great scattering of the early church, but this evil strategy to shut down the Jesus movement in the end only catalysed the next wave of missionary expansion. Wherever these Jesus-followers went they proclaimed the good news of the kingdom, extending the influence of the church into the regions surrounding Jerusalem.

Samaria

At the time of this great scattering Philip was directed by the Spirit, north, to Samaria. Samaritans, descendants of the Northern Kingdom, were seen by the Jews as compromisers. In the years after exile, very clear borders between Jews and Samaritans were established – geographical, theological and ethnic. Despite their once-shared ancestry a sectarian spirit raged. Jews didn't like their 'mixed-race' Samaritan neighbours, and the feeling was mutual!

Those like Philip, though, who had yielded to the Spirit, would get caught up in God's dramatic plan of salvation for the Samaritans.[17] Like a lightning rod attracting the power of heaven, Philip's proclamation of Jesus in the city of Samaria resulted in all sorts of kingdom breakthroughs. Demons were cast out, the sick were healed and great joy broke out across the city. Peter and John travelled to Samaria to see with their own eyes what Philip had catalysed. All they had heard was true. God's love was extending throughout the world. God's grace was untamed. The Spirit was truly moving.

God was not finished with Philip. He was caught up in another Holy Spirit directive, 'Go south to the road – the desert road.'[18] No one could have predicted that what Philip would encounter in the desert would be a chariot of African royalty. Prompted by the Spirit, Philip ran alongside the chariot and discovered that the traveller was the treasurer to the Queen of Ethiopia and happened to be reading from the scroll of the prophet Isaiah. God was chasing down the life of this man in a stunning act of 'boundary-transgressing love'.[19] As a eunuch, this traveller signified the margins of society. Distinguished by the colour of his dark skin and stigmatized by his sexuality, he represented the ultimate slave, a body familiar with use and abuse. Yet God was drawing this man close. Philip climbed into the chariot and began to explain the text the eunuch was reading, Isaiah 53:

> He was led like a lamb to the slaughter,
>   and as a sheep before its shearers is silent,
>   so he did not open his mouth.[20]

Philip described to the Ethiopian the good news. Jesus had suffered shame and humiliation so he didn't have to. He received the news with great joy and he took gospel joy back to Africa with him.

The Ethiopian eunuch would no longer remain on the margins. He had been drawn into the kingdom family.

This was where he belonged.

The Damascus Road

It's interesting that Luke transitions us from the story of the eunuch to the story of a man called Saul. These characters couldn't be any more different – one a marginalized slave serving a pagan empire, the other a religious fanatic holding strictly to the Mosaic law. Yet both these characters were arrested by divine desire as they travelled; the eunuch on the Desert Road, Saul on the Damascus Road.

Saul was a persecutor of the early church. He viewed followers of Jesus, like Stephen, with contempt. For Saul they were part of a rebellious sect, an enemy to true Judaism. Purging these rebels from Israel was a righteous act. Yet Luke's storytelling is revealing. Like Jesus, these followers had done nothing wrong. Saul was persecuting the innocent. In Acts chapter 9 we find Saul seeking legal permission to round up Christians in Damascus. Despite his resistance to the works of God, Saul was *wanted* by God. God's longing love would follow Saul to Damascus without his permission.

'Suddenly a light from heaven flashed around him.'[21] Saul fell to the ground. As he lay prostrate on the ground, an audible voice questioned him: 'Saul, Saul, why do you persecute me?'[22]

Imagine Saul, so convinced he had been serving God, confronted by these words. He did not know what was happening but he knew enough to realize this was sacred space. Yahweh was speaking. Saul replied, 'Who are you, Lord?'

'I am Jesus, whom you are persecuting,'[23] was the reply.

This was the astonishing revelation Saul could not previously bring himself to acknowledge. Yahweh, Israel's one true God, *is* Jesus! The further revelation for Saul was that Jesus and his Church were one. 'I am Jesus, whom you are persecuting' – Saul had to realize that when he persecuted followers of Jesus he was persecuting God. Only a revelation by the Spirit of the Lord could break Saul's fundamentalism. Saul had now 'heard the voice of a crucified God'[24] and it wrecked him. He would never be the same again. God was about to give Saul a new assignment:

Now get up and go into the city, and you will be told what you must do.[25]

Saul had to make his way to Damascus still blinded by his encounter of heavenly light. For three days unable to see, imagine Saul hour after hour replaying those sacred words of the Damascus Road in his mind. During those 72 hours he could only meditate on the last thing he had witnessed: the glory of Jesus.

At the end of these days a faithful saint called Ananias was summoned by the Spirit to go and lay hands on Saul. Given Saul's reputation, Ananias was understandably nervous, but convinced by the Lord's words he obeyed. 'Go! This man is my chosen instrument to proclaim my name to the Gentiles and their kings and to the people of Israel.'[26] As Ananias placed his hands on Saul, his eyes were opened and he was filled with the Holy Spirit. From this point on Saul would be known as Paul. A new identity was coming upon him for the radical shift that the trajectory of his life would now follow. Think about how wild this was – Saul the ultra-conservative, nationalistic Jew would become Paul, God's chosen instrument to the Gentiles. The scene was set for the next wave of gospel expansion but first The God Story switches the focus from Paul back to Peter.

The Gentile Pentecost

Peter had been on kingdom business. He had eventually based himself in Joppa where he stayed in the house of a tanner called Simon. A life-changing revelation awaited him there. First, though, Luke had to connect Peter with another 'unlikely' character who was about to be thrust into the centre of The God Story plot: a Roman centurion called Cornelius. How could these two lives be connected?

Cornelius was a contradiction – a man of war, bound to the Roman Empire yet a God-fearer who prayed and gave to the poor. God wanted Cornelius to know he was paying attention. During his time of prayer an angel appeared to Cornelius. 'Cornelius, God has heard your prayer and remembered your gifts to the poor,' the angel said. 'Send to Joppa for . . . Peter. He is a guest in the home of Simon the tanner, who lives by the sea.'[27]

Cornelius' life was about to be joined with Peter's in a stunning orchestration of the Spirit of God. A man familiar with instructions, Cornelius acted straight away and sent two servants to get Peter. Peter meanwhile was back at Simon's house relaxing on the rooftop. While someone downstairs was making Peter food, he fell into a trance. Peter saw a large sheet covering the whole earth coming down from heaven. On the sheet were all types of animals – clean and unclean, common and uncommon. God said, 'Get up, Peter. Kill and eat.'[28] Peter couldn't bring himself to do it. To eat these animals would be an outright violation of the law of Moses. '"Surely not, Lord!" Peter replied. "I have never eaten anything impure or unclean."'[29]

God spoke again. 'Do not call anything impure that God has made clean.'[30] Wow! Something radical was happening. Three times

God showed Peter this in the trance. Then the sheet returned to heaven.

Peter awoke. Shellshocked. *What just happened? What was God trying to tell me?*

A revolution had come down from heaven on this sheet and the boundaries of clean and unclean were being completely redrawn. The distinctions of purity that Peter had previously understood were now being expanded to include not just new food but new people. The table had just got bigger. Much bigger. A new world was being imagined and God had spoken a new word, definitively, to declare it so.

As Peter took stock of what he had just witnessed, Cornelius' servants made it to Simon's house and introduced themselves to Simon. God spoke to Peter, 'Three men are looking for you. So get up and go downstairs. Do not hesitate to go with them, for I have sent them.'[31]

Peter may not have had the full picture of what God was doing yet but he knew God was doing something. He left Simon's house and embarked on a journey to Cornelius' house with these men. Former strangers, now walking side by side into the purposes of God together.

As Peter arrived at Cornelius' house a large crowd was waiting for him. Curiosity and anticipation filled the air. Peter could sense it. He was about to step across the threshold of a Gentile household, not to mention into the home of a Roman centurion. Should this even be happening? Yet the Spirit inside Peter was compelling him. Divine desire was urging him forward and Peter knew it. The powerful love of God was about to break down every racial wall and upend every existing cultural code.

Cornelius welcomed those present. Peter listened to Cornelius describe his angelic visitation a few days previously and became convinced the moment unfolding before them was a sovereign plan of God. Peter opened his mouth and began to speak. 'I now realize how true it is God does not show favouritism but accepts from every nation the one who fears him and does what is right.'[32]

Peter knew God's promise to Abraham all those years ago was

being fulfilled right before his eyes. Peter preached Jesus and the forgiveness of sins that comes through his life and death. But God couldn't wait until Peter's sermon was through. Longing love had waited long enough. The Spirit fell. Cornelius' house would be the site of another Pentecost. The full force of the Father's love was stretching out over *all humanity*.

Those gathered began to speak in tongues and praise the Lord just like the 120 in the upper room had in Jerusalem. Peter could only confirm, 'They have received the Holy Spirit just as we have.'[33]

Of course, news spread quickly. The Gentiles had received the same Holy Spirit?! It was too much for some to take in. Peter went back to the mother-church in Jerusalem to confirm what God had allowed him to be a part of. While most of the believers celebrated what God was doing, some were critical and resistant. A spirit of control flared up which tried to stifle the new thing God was doing beyond Jerusalem. The wind of the Spirit was blowing more indiscriminately than some would have liked it to. Nevertheless, the Spirit's longing for all flesh would mean seeds of the gospel would be blown to places far beyond the Jewish boundaries.

One of the most significant of these was Antioch.

Antioch – a new home for the movement

Antioch was a city 300 miles north of Jerusalem. Many Christians who had been scattered through the persecution had ended up in this vibrant and ethnically diverse city. The fire of God was burning strong in these courageous Jesus-followers, and as they proclaimed the kingdom among the Gentiles they witnessed a wonderful move of God's Spirit. 'A great number of people believed and turned to the Lord.'[34]

The believers in Antioch grew to embody the life of Christ so vividly that it was here the nickname 'Christian' (Christlike Ones) was first coined. This was the first major city outside Jewish territory where Christianity gained a significant foothold. Antioch became a hub for all kinds of Holy Spirit activity. The city's ethnic diversity was reflected in the church and God would use this cosmopolitan city as the ideal launching pad for more kingdom expansion. It was also the perfect place for Paul to be reintroduced into the story.

Paul had endured a long period of time in the wilderness. The Damascus Road encounter had changed his life forever, but his interpretation of the Scriptures needed time to catch up. Picture Paul during those years poring over the Hebrew Scriptures alone with God. As the Spirit brought illumination, imagine the neurons in his brain firing together as he realized the sacred words and themes he had known his whole life had all been fulfilled in Jesus, his brilliant theological mind completely rewired by the Holy Spirit. Now he was ready to return. Antioch's cultural nerve-centre was the best fit for this Greek-speaking Jew and master-craftsman of the Scriptures. Paul, along with his friend Barnabas, poured himself into the Antioch church for a year, and as a result it flourished.

The leaders who had gathered in Antioch began to discern how a strategic hub to connect and resource the growing movement of churches was emerging. As they lifted up their holy ambition to God in prayer a fresh revelation of God's eternal purposes was revealed to them. 'While they were worshipping the Lord and fasting, the Holy Spirit said, "Set apart for me Barnabas and Saul for the work to which I have called them."'[35]

The church at Antioch was being caught up in the dream of God. The longing of the Spirit would be released through the hands of God's people. 'So after they had fasted and prayed, they placed their hands on them and sent them off.'[36]

A fresh gust of wind had come upon the flames burning in Antioch, and as Paul and Barnabas walked off into the unknown, a wildfire of God's love was about to be spread abroad in the nations.

Ends of the earth

From this point on Paul would play a leading role in the unfolding of the Great Commission. As divine desire for all peoples pulsed through Paul's being, he found himself venturing into new lands and cultures declaring to those 'who once were far off' 'the unsearchable riches of Christ'.[37] The wholly surrendered nature of Paul's life and his complete dependency on the grace of God made him a living vessel through which the power of God could flow. As he followed in the footsteps of Jesus, supernatural signs and wonders followed him as he boldly proclaimed the gospel of the kingdom.

In Paul's first missionary journey the wind of the Spirit blew him to towns and small cities in Cyprus and Galatia (modern-day Turkey). As Paul shared the good news, a sorcerer was blinded, a governor was converted, a lame man was healed and many were filled with the Spirit. The resistance, however, was real. Many Jews responded angrily to Paul's claims of Jesus over and above Moses. Stoned and left for dead, Paul would get up and go again, embodying the love of Jesus in a staggering display of forgiveness and courage.

Years later Paul was carried off again by the Spirit into new frontiers, but his strategic intention to take the gospel further into Asia was interrupted by a supernatural dream. A Macedonian man appeared to Paul in the night, calling out, 'Come over to Macedonia and help us.'[38] Concluding that this call to what we now know as Europe was an orchestration of the Spirit, Paul set sail for Philippi, the leading city of Macedonia and a Roman colony. When he arrived, all sorts of breakthroughs opened up before him.

Salvation. Individuals were converted to Christ. The Lord had prepared the heart of a businesswoman named Lydia. As Paul opened his mouth to declare the good news, the Spirit opened up her heart to receive Jesus.

Deliverance. Demons were driven out. A slave girl in the city who was forced by her abusive employers to fortune-tell was set free by Paul's death-defeating words of authority.

Justice. Not only was this slave girl set free but also the unjust system taking advantage of her was dismantled when those who had controlled her realized they could no longer make their money from her.

Freedom. Thrown in jail because of their kingdom mischief in Philippi, Paul and his co-worker Silas decided to worship God from their prison cell. As they lifted their voices in song, the foundations of the jail were shaken and the chains of all the prisoners were loosed. Paul and Silas walked out of the prison free, but not before they had led the bewildered and fearful prison guard to Christ.

Churches planted. As Paul left Philippi, at least two house churches had been planted. Lydia's home and the prison guard's household had become locations of the new kingdom family.

The wind of the Spirit blowing through Philippi had carried the sound of freedom. What happened in Philippi would be repeated in different ways in significant places like Thessalonica, Corinth, Athens and Ephesus. Paul and his friends became known as those 'who have turned the world upside down'.[39] As they followed the Spirit's lead they catalysed wholesale transformation in these cities, rewriting the false narratives which had defined them for far too long. Idols would be exposed, chains would be broken, principalities and powers would be displaced and churches would be planted.

A family of families

These new churches would face huge challenges. How could this multicultural, diverse body of churches, spiralling across the Roman Empire, stay true to Jesus and the teachings of the kingdom? Paul would give his life for this task. When he couldn't get to the churches in person he pored over letters he would write to them. His letters taught them how to be a people animated by the Spirit of God. Paul's commitment was to show the churches how life in the kingdom of God applied to every corner of human existence – how to follow Jesus *in all of life.* Paul therefore applied the gospel to a breadth of issues: from speaking in tongues to marriage counselling; from the issues surrounding circumcision to how new believers should treat their unbelieving spouses; from issues of sexuality to how to engage with a pagan government and their daily work. The challenges were complex and the pressure was intense, yet through the revelation of the Spirit Paul had become convinced these young churches, despite all their imperfections, were revealing God's eternal purposes to the world. The Church was the means through which the multifaceted, kaleidoscopic nature of God's wisdom and beauty would be displayed to the universe. Paul knew bringing this truth into the open was the reason God had ambushed him that day on the Damascus Road. There has never been any other community or citizenship on the earth like the Church. A people transcending every cultural barrier, joined not by status or nationality, but by belief in a crucified God, Jesus Christ.

God had also graced Paul with a special ability to hold this growing web of churches and kingdom partnerships together. He helped create a living network of relationships, teaching the churches how to mutually submit to one another and resource one another. From house-church leaders like Chloe in Corinth and Lydia in Philippi to civil servants like Erastus and doctors like Luke; from co-workers like Priscilla and Aquila to sons in the faith like Timothy and Titus; from former slaves like Onesimus and Tertius to wealthy patrons like Jason and Phoebe; all these and many more played their part in a family of families spreading across the world.

This explains why, beyond Paul's outstanding theological skill, it was his tone that stood out most in his letters. Paul referred to those he was addressing as his siblings, his children, his friends. He likened his loving concern for them to that of a mother and father. He was bound together with them by the Spirit. Paul constantly carried these vulnerable but courageous communities in his heart. He was fiercely committed to the churches but never heavy handed, firm at times but always gentle. And he never stopped praying for them.

Rome

After approximately 30 years and 10,000 miles of travelling, Paul had journeyed through Israel, Syria, Asia Minor, Malta, Cyprus, Crete, Macedonia and Italy. But he was not done. Acts reveals the wind of the Spirit would finally blow him all the way to Rome. Despite almost losing his life a number of times Paul made it to what many believed was the centre of civilization and the heart of the Gentile world. Constrained by the authorities and placed under house arrest, at first glance it appears the book of Acts ends in anticlimactic fashion: 'For two whole years Paul stayed there in his own rented house and welcomed all who came to see him.'[40] But we must read the next verse too, for Luke has juxtaposed this picture of constraint with one more sentence, the final words of Acts: 'He proclaimed the kingdom of God and taught about the Lord Jesus Christ – with all boldness and without hindrance!'[41]

Paul may have been confined to a room in Rome, but the gospel would go forth without hindrance! The open-ended finale to Acts was deliberate. The words of Jesus – *Jerusalem, Judea, Samaria, to the ends of the earth* – had come true. The gospel had made its way into the heart of the empire, but it would not stop there. The dream of the Trinity before the foundations of the world had come to pass. People from all backgrounds and nations – rich and poor, Jew and Gentile, male and female, master and slave – had been formed in family through the fiery love of the Spirit. Unified around the bread and cup and embodying the sacrificial love of Jesus, nothing could contain the power latent in the kingdom family. A holy temple of living stones had now become the place of God's habitation. The Spirit had found a new home in Jesus' body on the earth.

The Church.

Presence: The Church is a movement of the Spirit, God's own personal presence. At Pentecost the disciples were baptized by the Spirit and immersed in God's love and power. From this point on every person acknowledging Jesus as Lord and yielding to him would be filled with God on the inside. Flash-flooded by the Spirit, the Church was empowered to continue Jesus' mission on the earth as presence-people! God's new home on earth was a temple made of living stones where his presence would dwell.

Family: Jesus formed a new family on the earth. A holy community revealing the Eternal Family's dream from the beginning. The Spirit was binding the disciples deep as a kindred family. They would learn to love one another like Jesus. What started as a small Jewish community would grow to become a diverse multi-ethnic global family united in Jesus. Led by the apostles, the Church came to understand itself as Christ's body on the earth, each believer a member playing a crucial part. As they multiplied throughout the world they came to understand themselves as a spiralling family of families. And as they did they unveiled the mystery of God's manifold wisdom to the world: the Church.

Kingdom: The Church is a colony of heaven. A community that both acts as a signpost to the eternal kingdom to come and demonstrates that kingdom availability now. Jesus is building his Church and the kingdom of darkness will not prevail against it. This is what Pentecost was all about. God in all flesh. Those who love Jesus can walk in the power of the Spirit – proclaiming the kingdom with their words, embodying the kingdom through their acts of mercy and demonstrating the kingdom through signs and wonders.

Father, thank you that you want to fill us with your Spirit, to flash-flood our lives with your love and power. Holy Spirit, baptize us with your fire once again. Father, thank you for forging us into a beautiful community of brothers and sisters from every tribe and tongue, the greatest movement the world has ever known.

Questions for reflection: Why don't you ask the Holy Spirit to fill and baptize you afresh right now? How is the community of the Church different from any other community or citizenship that has ever existed? How can the church family I am a part of more fully proclaim, embody and demonstrate God's Kingdom to the watching world around us.

11

The Revelation

Approximately 60 years after the Church was birthed, the apostle John found himself banished to a Greek island called Patmos under the reign of the Roman Emperor Domitian. And, holed up in a cave on this remote piece of land, John received a heavenly vision.

John's circumstances, naturally speaking, meant his influence on the early churches was redundant. He was completely isolated from their growing movement throughout the Roman Empire. Yet what he was about to behold would not only influence the Church in every succeeding generation but also define how history itself would unfold.

Caught up in the Spirit, John initially heard a voice like the sound of rushing waters, instructing him to write down what he saw. As he turned towards the voice he saw a Man walking among seven lampstands. Looking closer, he saw the Man was adorned in dazzling splendour. His eyes were burning with fire and his face was shining as bright as the sun. John knew he was encountering the glorious and exalted Jesus. Remember, John had spent three years walking with Jesus during his time on earth. He knew Jesus as well as anyone. Yet this fresh encounter moved John from familiar to fascinated. The one who had laid his head on Jesus' chest now lay before his exalted Lord like a dead man. John's fear dissipated with Jesus' first words, 'Do not be afraid.'[1]

Isn't this what God has been saying to humanity from the Fall? *Don't be afraid . . .*

Jesus continues:

I am the First and the Last. I am the Living One; I was dead, and now look, I am alive for ever and ever! And I hold the keys of death and Hades.

Write, therefore, what you have seen, what is now and what will take place later.[2]

Jesus was peeling back heaven, about to unveil to one of his most trusted friends a stratospheric vision of reality from heaven's perspective. This is what the word 'revelation' means: 'an unveiling', 'a showing', 'a revealing'.

But the revelation wasn't just for John. This vivid picture of Jesus walking among seven lampstands was a symbol of his ongoing presence among the churches in Asia. John was tasked with passing the message on.

To many modern readers Revelation is a complex book, for it is a mixture of apocalyptic, prophetic and pastoral genres. But this was a form of first-century Jewish literature many of its readers would have been familiar with. Further, the symbols and numbers are all drawn from the Old Testament, encouraging the early Christians to connect their present reality to rich themes of The God Story. Revelation is not a secret predictive code we have to crack to work out when the world will end. It is first and foremost a letter to encourage the early churches in their cultural context. Despite all the speculative end-time controversies connected with Revelation, it is a book written in real time, to real Christians who were part of actual churches in the first century. Ephesus, Smyrna, Pergamum, Thyatira, Sardis, Philadelphia, Laodicea. In each of these cities real flesh-and-blood people like us gathered together as the kingdom family.

The recurring theme at the heart of Jesus' message to the churches was *don't give in and don't give up, I am with you*. In truth, the seven churches were characterized by a mixture of faithfulness and compromise, by apathy and courage, by sacrifice and selfishness. John would go on to record Jesus speaking words of comfort and challenge to each of the seven churches spread throughout Asia. Jesus wanted them to know that he had not forgotten the promise he made to those first disciples, 'I am with you always, to the very end of the age.'[3] John's opening words convey this underlying sense of solidarity the revelation of Jesus to his Church is all about:

I, John, your brother and companion in the suffering and kingdom and patient endurance that are ours in Jesus . . .[4]

Pressure

The sheer level of kingdom advancement the Church had experienced during the first century is staggering given the pressure they had to endure. The influences of the 'dark trinity' were acutely experienced: the powerful seduction of the intimidating idolatrous culture they lived within (the world); the age-old temptations of the self-centred nature (the flesh); and the deceptive tactics of Satan and his pagan empires wielding cruel persecution (the devil).

Domitian was the Roman emperor (Caesar) for most of the last two decades of the first century. Under his reign some of the fiercest attacks on Christians were implemented. Domitian had demanded universal worship. Once a year, before his own sculpture, incense was thrown on an altar fire while his subjects exclaimed, 'Caesar is Lord.' To refuse this form of empire allegiance had consequences. But to counter this with the bold pronouncement 'Jesus is Lord' was a matter of life and death.

The malevolent forces of the world, the flesh and the devil buffeted the early church from every side, threatening to extinguish the fire of the Spirit burning at the centre of their communities. Being under pressure was 'normal' for the first Jesus-followers. The world's rival systems and powers hated them like Jesus said would happen. Pressure was not something they wanted or asked for, but it was something they expected. Jesus had told the disciples, 'In this world you will have trouble.'[5] The word for 'trouble', often translated 'tribulation' or 'suffering', is used 18 times in the New Testament. The Greek word for this is '*thlipsis*', which gets at the idea of something or someone being compressed, hemmed in or constricted. *Thlipsis* = Pressure!

Jesus had also warned the disciples things would get worse before they would get better. A great tribulation would come and all of the created order would experience the pressure of the inbreaking of God's kingdom colliding with the kingdom of darkness. Jesus had described the effects of this collision as birth pains moving through creation, predicting signs such as divisions, war and famine.[6]

The apostles, under the inspiration of the Spirit, developed a theological framework to help the early church live through the pressure this collision had produced. This was one of the main purposes of their letters. How could those who loved Jesus stay true to his teachings despite the fierce challenges and persecution pressing upon them?

Three things about the apostles' instructions to the churches stand out.

First of all, the Church needed to understand the kingdom Jesus came declaring was both a present reality and a future fulfilment. Jesus had inaugurated the kingdom of God on the earth through his life, death, resurrection and ascension. God's will and God's ways were already breaking into earth. But only through the return of Jesus would the complete establishment and full enjoyment of God's rule and reign be realized. The kingdom was therefore both a 'now and not-yet' reality and the Church had to learn how to live in this tension.

The apostle Paul developed Jesus' birth pains metaphor to describe how this tension had given voice to an ache resident in the very fabric of creation:

We know that the whole creation has been groaning as in the pains of childbirth right up to the present time.[7]

The Fall had brought a curse upon creation, subjecting it to decay. Yet something deep within the fabric of creation knew a glorious liberty now awaited it. The groaning of a new birth had begun. Remarkably, then, Paul connected the coming liberty of creation to the full release of humankind:

For the creation waits in eager expectation for the children of God to be revealed.[8]

It is startling to think that creation will only be released into its eternal liberty when the sons and daughters of God experience the fullness of theirs. In other words, the Church groans in sync with the soul of creation:

> Not only so, but we ourselves, who have the firstfruits of the Spirit, groan inwardly as we wait eagerly for our adoption to sonship, the redemption of our bodies.[9]

Paul was helping the early Jesus-followers construct a mature worldview of the kingdom of God in the age they were living in. The God Story's spectacular finale will only come when both creation and humankind are released into their glorious destiny together. This will bring about the ultimate restoration of spirit and matter, when everything that has been corrupted through the Fall is restored in the end.

Second, Paul, like the other apostles, wanted the early church to know the Holy Spirit specializes in helping us through this now and not-yet tension. In fact, this deep longing for full redemption was an inward work of the Holy Spirit within them. So on the days when it was hard and the pressure was relentless, these first believers could take confidence in the fact that the Spirit was closer than ever. Knowing them better than they knew themselves, the Spirit would pray through God's sons and daughters when they couldn't find the words.[10] He would take their wordless groans and offer them up before the Father who loved them:

> In the same way, the Spirit helps us in our weakness. We do not know what we ought to pray for, but the Spirit himself intercedes for us through wordless groans. And he who searches our hearts knows the mind of the Spirit, because the Spirit intercedes for God's people in accordance with the will of God.[11]

Third, and flowing from these first two points, the early believers of the first churches needed to be reminded there was a divine purpose in the pressure. The world, the flesh and the devil would do their best to squeeze the Church into submission. Yet, as the believers opened up their lives to the Spirit, somehow they would be enlarged. Suffering, as painful as it may be, would allow a process of transformation to take place that couldn't happen in any other way. The apostle James, brother of Jesus, captures it beautifully:

> Consider it a sheer gift, friends, when tests and challenges come at you from all sides. You know that under pressure, your faith-life is forced into the open and shows its true colours. So don't try to get out of anything prematurely. Let it do its work so you become mature . . .[12]

Somehow in this painful process, even what had been designed for evil would be turned for good and God's eternal purposes.

A throne-ward vision

When everything around the early Jesus-followers was shaking and the pressure they were experiencing was building, they needed to see Jesus. Revelation was all about inviting a persecuted and vulnerable Church to come up higher, to see a greater reality, to be moved again by the beauty of Jesus. The Vision is always Jesus.

John's vision had started with seeing the exalted Jesus. But now he was invited even further into glorious mystery. John's eyes were drawn to an open door standing before him, then a voice like the sound of a trumpet called out to him, 'Come up here, and I will show you what must take place.'[13]

John walked through the door. Let's enter in with him.

Immediately John was caught up in a supreme display of magnificent worship. Before him was the throne of God, dazzling in radiant beauty and splendour. A rainbow that shone like an emerald encircled the throne of God, and surrounding the throne were 24 elders dressed in white, all with crowns of gold upon their heads. These 24 elders who were sitting on 24 thrones represented the 12 tribes of Israel and the 12 disciples – the new Israel, the Church. From the throne came peals of thunder and flashes of lighting, and in front of the throne was a sea of glass as clear as crystal. Seven lamps shone brightly. Seven, the biblical number of completion and perfection, based on God's creation cycle, is woven into every part of this book.

Moving around the throne were four living creatures – a lion, an ox, one with a human face, and an eagle – and together they cried out, '"Holy, holy, holy is the Lord God Almighty," who was, and is, and is to come.'[14] Fascinated forever and unable to fully comprehend the beauty of God's glory, the living creatures sing this song unceasingly day and night.

As they worshipped, the 24 elders joined in unison. Overwhelmed by God's wonder and grandeur they cast their crowns before him, falling down and bowing before him.

Caught up in this atmosphere of unceasing worship, John saw in the right hand of the One on the throne, a scroll sealed with seven seals. At this point an angel cried out, 'Who is worthy to break the seals and open the scroll?'[15] No one could be found to answer this question and something collapsed inside John. It seemed like something deep was broken in the universe. The scroll symbolized the unfolding of history and someone of authority needed to open it to guide history to its divine conclusion.

But no one could be found worthy to open it.

John wept and wept.

At this point an elder came to comfort John. 'Do not weep!' the elder said. 'See, the Lion of the tribe of Judah, the Root of David, has triumphed. He is able to open the scroll and its seven seals.'[16] John would have been familiar with these words. They were packed with themes relating to the ancient prophecies of a messianic king, one who would come to bring about a great conquest like King David had, leading God's people into freedom. As John received these comforting words, imagine his hopes begin to rise. The Messiah has triumphed. God has kept his covenant promise – a Davidic king will sit on the throne forever. He can open the scroll! But as John paid careful attention to what was unfolding, he saw not a great warrior but a Lamb, standing at the centre of the throne.

A Lamb bloodied. A Lamb which appeared to have been slain. With the eyes of all the heavenly hosts fixed upon this Lamb, it moved forward towards the throne and took the scroll.

Pause for a moment as you imagine what happened next. The 24 elders and the living creatures, now joined by tens of thousands of angels, began bowing down and worshipping the Lamb. They began to sing in a loud voice:

Worthy is the Lamb, who was slain,
> to receive power and wealth and wisdom and strength
> and honour and glory and praise![17]

John was undone. In these moments everything he had come to know about the humble and sacrificial Jesus on the earth was confirmed in this glorious experience of heaven. This exalted vision left him in no doubt who the true King of the heavens and the earth really was. The Lion of Judah, the Great Deliverer, was a slain Lamb.

This revelation of the throne room was therefore an exhortation to the churches not to be seduced by the way the world understands power. God had not made his way to his throne the way other kings do, on a great white horse, surrounded by the cheers of his armies. God made his way to his throne alone, like a lamb going to the slaughterhouse. The God of the heavens being crucified on a Roman cross was a scandalous claim. Yet this act of sacrificial love was the most powerful act history has ever known. And the churches were called to embody this same love.

They may have been surrounded by the empire ideology and threat, but the one who was really ruling over the universe is a meek, crucified God. Sacrificial Love had dismantled every other empire. One of the mighty angels, later in John's vision, confirms it: 'The kingdom of the world has become the kingdom of our Lord and of his Messiah, and he will reign for ever and ever.'[18]

This is the ultimate direction of The God Story plot. All of history is on a throne-ward trajectory heading towards the feet of the humble resurrected King, Jesus!

Patient endurance

Imagine the encouragement this powerful picture of the throne room would have been for the early churches. Ponder them joining in with the angels worshipping the Lamb of God as they received John's revelation. Think about how it would have encouraged them to stay true to the Way of Jesus in the midst of a power-hungry, idolatrous culture.

This majestic view of Jesus ruling over the nations and the way it stirred worship powerfully enabled the primary purpose of Revelation to be fulfilled: the patient endurance of the saints.

John's opening words of Revelation to the churches had made this purpose clear: 'patient endurance that [is] ours in Jesus'.[19] The theme is repeated throughout the book. Seven times in total the words 'patient endurance' are used. Four of these times Jesus uses it to exhort the churches of Asia. On two other occasions as John's vision unfolds he boldly states the whole point of the revelation is to call the Church to patient endurance:

> Here is a call for the endurance of the saints, those who keep the commandments of God and their faith in Jesus.[20]

Add to this exhortations towards patient endurance from Jesus, Paul, Peter, James, Timothy, Titus and the writer to the Hebrews and we begin to realize this often undervalued virtue was a central characteristic of the early church.

Patiently enduring the pressures surrounding them was the way the early church made sense of the 'now and not-yet' reality of the kingdom of God. It was the way the first Jesus-followers kept the fire in their hearts burning despite the resistance they were experiencing. Counterintuitively, it was the way, even through suffering, their joyful anticipation deepened.

The early church exemplified patient endurance in a way that seems foreign to our twenty-first-century consumerist culture. But it was also a peculiar characteristic when viewed against the first-century culture the early Christians were living in. Alan

Kreider says, 'Patience was not a virtue dear to most Greco-Roman people, and it has been of little interest to modern scholars of early Christianity. But it was centrally important to the early Christians.'

Kreider continues, 'The Christians believed that God is patient and that Jesus visibly embodied patience.'[21] Patience was therefore a key virtue to the earliest Jesus-followers and a key characteristic of their church communities. The early kingdom families endured together. As they clung to God they clung to one another, bearing one another's burdens, crying one another's tears, exhorting one another to faithfulness, reminding one another through multiple acts of kindness not to give up, not to give in.

Patient endurance is not simply self-strength or gutting it out in a way that denies or minimizes pain. It is the opposite of anxious, forceful, controlling behaviour. Rather, this fruit of the Spirit is how we channel our passion for Jesus into wholehearted trust in the Father's unfolding plan when we don't know exactly what that will mean for us.

The apostle Paul's words to the church in Rome describe how this spiritual formation process takes place:

> We rejoice in our sufferings [*thlipsis*, pressure], knowing that suffering produces endurance, and endurance produces character, and character produces hope, and hope does not put us to shame, because God's love has been poured into our hearts through the Holy Spirit who has been given to us.[22]

As the early church allowed themselves to be formed in this virtue they became a faithful, non-anxious presence in the midst of a pagan culture. Their witness revealed patient endurance is not a weak mode of survival but humble strength, the means through which the Church overcomes and the kingdom of God multiplies in the world.

Running the race

The author of Hebrews reminds us that patient endurance has been the standout characteristic of all the great characters of

The God Story. In chapter 11, the author records names and snapshots of people like Noah, Abraham, Sarah, Isaac, Jacob, Moses, Rahab and Gideon. Highlighting their faith in action when God's promises seemed obscure and distant, the author wants to inspire the Church to endure despite the pressure and uncertainty surrounding their lives – to develop a confidence that when we are unsure of what the future holds, we know the embrace of the One we will endure it with. These women and men relentlessly anchored their trust in the unshakeable faithfulness of God.

The writer to the Hebrews climaxes the description of these faithful saints by using the metaphor of running a race. As the early church takes up her role in the chapters of The God Story yet to be written, the author wants them to imagine themselves surrounded by a great crowd of those who have gone before, cheering them on towards the finish line, where Jesus awaits us:

Therefore, since we are surrounded by such a great cloud of witnesses, let us throw off everything that hinders and the sin that so easily entangles. And let us run with perseverance [patient endurance] the race marked out for us, fixing our eyes on Jesus, the pioneer and perfecter of faith. For the joy set before him he endured the cross, scorning its shame, and sat down at the right hand of the throne of God. Consider him who endured such opposition from sinners, so that you will not grow weary and lose heart.[23]

Jesus was the ultimate example of endurance. As a human being he patiently endured for his fellow humanity. Jesus went through what we could never imagine enduring: the physical torture, the utter shame and the anguished separation from the Father on the cross.

Yet, almost incomprehensibly, it was joy that helped Jesus endure this painstaking agony. He carried a picture of the finish line in sight: people from every tribe and tongue and nation gathered around the throne as one family. The dream of the Eternal Family from the beginning undiminished in Jesus' heart inspired him to go to hell and back for us. Take a moment to ponder this humbling reality: we are the joyful reward that carried Jesus through his suffering.

The early church, inspired by the endurance of Jesus and cheered on by the saints of old, fixed their eyes on the finish line and kept running. The first disciples led the way. Jesus had called them his 'witnesses'. The original meaning of this word is 'martyr'. As we read of how their lives unfolded, we understand why.

The God Story records the details of the deaths of James, the brother of John, who was beheaded by Herod, and of Stephen whom we mentioned in the previous chapter. We rely on Christian tradition for records of the rest of the first disciples. Peter was crucified, upside down at his request, most likely in Rome. James, Jesus' younger brother and the leader of the church in Jerusalem, was eventually thrown off the pinnacle of the temple and then clubbed to death. Andrew carried the gospel to what is now Southern Russia, parts of modern-day Turkey and Greece, where it is thought he was crucified on an X-shaped cross. Thomas was active in the East, mostly likely as far as India, where he was pierced through with spears. Philip is thought to have had a ministry in North Africa before he went to modern-day Turkey, where he was hanged. Matthew carried the gospel to Persia (modern-day Iran), where he was slain by the sword. Bartholomew (Nathaniel) was flayed alive in Armenia, where Thaddeus was also shot with arrows. Simon, the former Zealot, ministered in Persia and was crucified after refusing to sacrifice to the sun god. Paul was beheaded in Rome.[24]

Thanks to the sacrificial exploits and patient endurance of each of these disciples, the mission of Jesus made phenomenal gains throughout the first century. But they weren't the only ones. The writer of the Hebrews reminds us they were joined by thousands of other passionate Jesus-followers who were prepared to leave everything and everyone to continue the mission of Jesus on the earth.

Revelation reveals how heaven rewards those who have endured, and will patiently endure, to such extremes. As John's throne-ward vision unfolded in chapters 6 and 7, his attention was caught by a multitude dressed in white robes around the throne. These were the ones who had come through great tribulation. John could hear the martyrs crying out, 'How long, Sovereign Lord . . . until you judge the inhabitants of the earth?'[25] as they longed for The God Story's final chapter to be fulfilled.

But they are told to wait a little longer.

The end is coming soon.

Jesus' return

The return of Jesus really was the great hope of the early church. A core part of the gospel message pointed to how Jesus would come a second time as rightful king to judge the living and the dead.[26] Jesus would vindicate his people, dealing with evil once and for all, establishing God's eternal kingdom of justice and righteousness. Jesus had told the disciples that the gospel of the kingdom would be preached in all nations and then the end of this present age would come.[27] No one could predict the exact moment of Jesus' return, but certain signs would indicate the return was close. One of these signs was that the love of many would grow cold.[28] To them, Jesus' return would bring about the sobering reality of eternal separation from Christ. However, to those who were actively waiting and prepared, the return of Jesus was an anchoring hope and inspiration to stay faithful to the end. Their names would be written in the Book of Life.[29]

The letters to the early churches were therefore punctuated with encouragement to be ready; to live in light of Jesus' soon return; to shine like stars in a twisted and corrupted world;[30] to be faithful in the tension of this in-between age. If they did they could be sure they would meet Jesus in the air at his return. Paul had taught them that a great resurrection of bodies would take place. The dead in Christ would rise from their graves and those still alive would be caught up to be with Jesus. In the end a divine upgrade of their bodies was coming. Because Jesus' victory had swallowed up death, mortality would be swapped for immortality![31] A resurrected body like Jesus' would be a reward for those who stayed faithful to the end.

For the first few decades of the Church's existence the first Christians lived off Jesus' words to the disciples before he was crucified. He was going to come back again. But as the apostles were martyred one by one and the majority of the first-generation Jesus-followers began to die, the succeeding generations of the Church needed more encouragement to anchor their hope in the future glory to come.

This is why the Revelation of Jesus to John, around the end of the first century, is so significant!

Making all things new

Revelation in its unique style connects the past, present and future together in Jesus Christ, 'the Alpha and the Omega, the Beginning and the End'.[32] In doing so it is the perfect conclusion to The God Story.

John brought rich images and themes of previous chapters of The God Story together in a tapestry of tremendous encouragement to the early church in their context. But in the final chapters of this book, Jesus would give John a wondrous vision of the future that would connect the Church across the ages together in a glorious destiny:

Then I saw 'a new heaven and a new earth', for the first heaven and the first earth had passed away, and there was no longer any sea. I saw the Holy City, the new Jerusalem, coming down out of heaven from God, prepared as a bride beautifully dressed for her husband. And I heard a loud voice from the throne saying, 'Look! God's dwelling place is now among the people, and he will dwell with them. They will be his people, and God himself will be with them and be their God. "He will wipe every tear from their eyes. There will be no more death" or mourning or crying or pain, for the old order of things has passed away.'

He who was seated on the throne said, 'I am making everything new!'[33]

The Maker of heaven and earth, who in the beginning created all that exists, is going to remake everything broken by the Fall. Creation, marred by sin, will be reborn.

Picture him reigning and ruling supreme, joyfully declaring over creation:

I am making all things new.

In the end it's all going to be OK. In the end there will only be a new beginning.

All shall be well, all shall be well, all manner of things shall be well.[34]

The old order is passing away. God is making EVERYTHING new. Bodies. Minds. Hearts. Relationships. Families. Cities. Creation. This exquisite picture of everlasting renewal draws together all the threads of The God Story in a perfect climax.

The story that started in a garden will end in a beautiful city. We will reign and rule with God in the new heaven and new earth. God's dream for the borders of Eden to be extended throughout the world will come to pass. The glory of God will cover the earth as the waters cover the sea.

I am making all things new.

There will be no more pain or suffering. Death will find its own grave. The pressure will end. Tears will be dried up. Sorrow will be no more. Sickness will be eliminated. Injustice will be ended. Satan will be completely vanquished.

The seed of promised blessing for all nations given to Abraham will flower into full bloom. A bride of all ethnic peoples, joined in glorious worship, will be prepared for their Bridegroom King. The Father will delight over his family. Heaven will be married to earth. There will only be *shalom*.

I am making all things new.

The Lamb at the centre of the throne will receive the reward of his suffering. Every knee will bow and every tongue will shout, Jesus is King, to the glory of God the Father.[35]

Face to face we will look into the eyes of Jesus, the Author and

Finisher of our story. Now we know in part, but then we will know, as we are fully known.[36] Love's greatest longing will be satisfied. The Eternal Family's dream will be realized. People from every tribe and tongue will join the dance.

God will be with them. They will be with God.

Home. Forever.

Come, Lord Jesus

Revelation has shown us how the pages of history will close and how eternity will unfold. It's no wonder the favourite prayer of the early church was, 'O Lord, Come.' John's beatific revelation of the fulfilment of the ages had only intensified their longing. *Maranatha* was how they said it in Aramaic and it became one of the earliest recorded heart-cries of the first Christians. The final words of Revelation close on this theme of Love's eternal longing. A Great Wedding is about to take place:

The Spirit and the bride say, 'Come!'[37]

These intimate words stretch across 2000 years of Church history. God in us is crying out to God beyond us. The Spirit knits us together with the prayers of the saints across the ages as we wait; walking in faith, anchored in hope and overflowing in love.

Revelation started with a vision of Jesus and ends with a longing for Jesus. In between, it confirms The God Story is one unified plotline leading to Jesus. The Vision is Jesus.

The early churches who heard John's revelation first have been joined with countless Christians down through the ages who cry out for the Bridegroom to return. Let our voices rise, joining the chorus of prayer from hearts overflowing with love:

Maranatha – come, Lord Jesus.

'Yes, I am coming soon,' Jesus replies.

Amen. Come, Lord Jesus.

The grace of the Lord Jesus be with God's people. Amen.[38]

Presence: As we await Jesus' return he calls us to patiently endure with the promise of his presence. Jesus reveals himself as the glorious, exalted Lord walking among the lampstands (churches). He reassures us he is with us in the pressure. As we receive fresh throne-ward vision of who Jesus is and the awesomeness of his presence we are moved from familiar to fascinated all over again. We only know in part but one day we will see him face to face. This is our anchoring hope. One day we will know as we are fully known in the perfection of his presence. God will dwell with humanity forever.

Family: As we lift our eyes above the pressure to worship Jesus we see people from every tribe and tongue surrounding the throne. God's dream will be fulfilled; representatives from every nation and family on the earth will be gathered around the throne. Every cultural barrier will be broken down, every relational hurt will be healed, every social class eroded. We will be one as the Eternal Family are one. In the meantime we endure together as the family of God, bearing one another's burdens. Joined with the Spirit we cry out together, *Come, Lord Jesus.*

Kingdom: The Revelation of Jesus reminds the Church that our destiny is to rule and reign with God in his eternal kingdom. A universal reign of peace will be established in the new heaven and earth. The opposing kingdom of darkness will be defeated once and for all. In the meantime the new creation project is moving through the nations and we have been handed the keys of the kingdom to help advance it. We walk and love in the way of the Lamb slain, the only one worthy to open the scroll, our Bridegroom King who will return soon for his bride. Until that time we pray as Jesus taught us.

Our Father in heaven, hallowed be your name, your kingdom come, your will be done, on earth as it is in heaven. Give us today our daily bread. And forgive us our debts, as we also have forgiven our debtors. And lead us not into temptation, but deliver us from the evil one. For yours is the kingdom, the power and the glory, forever and ever. Amen.

Questions for reflection: Are there any areas of your life where Jesus is encouraging you to 'come up higher' to receive fresh throne-ward vision? How does a vision of God's future kingdom inspire and empower you to live faithfully for Jesus in the present? How are you being invited to grow in patient endurance amid the pressures of life?

12

Conclusion: Stepping into the Story

The two years it has taken us to write this book have come after almost 20 years of friendship, walking with Jesus together like the two on the Emmaus Road. We are more convinced than ever that The God Story really is the story the whole world is waiting to hear. As this book ends, we carry three great hopes in our heart for you.

1 That you will know and love the Author

We didn't write this book to neatly tie up the Scriptures or reduce the drama of the Bible to a theological document. We wrote in the hope it will provoke a longing to know God in a radically intimate way. He is the Author and main character of the Story. There is no end to God and there is no end to his love, and we hope you will spend the rest of your days searching out the unsearchable riches of Jesus.

The two friends on the Emmaus Road knew a version of The God Story. In fact, they were well versed in much of it. But everything changed when the Author himself taught them it. It felt more personal. It was more real. It set their hearts on fire. What if we just need to hear the greatest story ever told by the greatest person who has ever lived?

Saint Augustine said many years ago, 'The single desire that dominated my search for delight was simply to love and be loved.'[1] Augustine came to realize that only something beyond us can complete us. The God Story affirms this primal longing within each human being but teaches us that first and foremost we are not the seekers or the lovers; rather we are the sought and the beloved. God's invitation to communion with him is the heart of The God Story. An invitation not primarily to intellectual ascent or behaviour modification but an invitation to *relationship*, to fall into his arms in loving surrender.

2 That you might find your story in God's big story

Alasdair MacIntyre famously said in his seminal book *After Virtue*: 'I can only answer the question, "What am I to do?" if I can answer the prior question, "Of what story or stories do I find myself part?"'[2] MacIntyre's profound statement above proposes that 'story' is hardwired into us as human beings. Why is it every time we hear the soft inviting phrase, 'Once upon a time', we are hooked, curious to know what the pregnant nature of these charming words will give birth to? Why do we love sitting around fires or kitchen tables with friends and family reliving and retelling stories from our lives ('Remember that time when . . .')? Why does social media encourage us to capture and present our lives as 'stories' to the watching online world? It seems something fundamental to our existence is exercised when we are drawn into a story. As human beings we are meaning-making creatures. Yet so often we struggle to make sense of the world and our place in it. What if MacIntyre is right? What if we can only understand our purpose in life by allowing the stories of our lives to find their place in a bigger and more beautiful story, one we are called to not merely read about but *participate in*?

Each one of our lives is a splendid never-to-be-repeated story of grace. Each one of our stories is precious and worthy of being told, shared and experienced. Yet none of our stories will make sense in isolation, disconnected from a wider plot. Think about all the best films. The roles of the individual characters, whether they are brilliant or broken, can only be understood within a bigger plot or storyboard. In a not dissimilar way, our real-life stories only truly find meaning when they are connected to the very source of our lives and the wider unfolding drama into which we were born.

Eugene Peterson summarizes the point beautifully:

When we submit our lives to what we read in scripture, we find that we are not being led to see God in our stories but our stories in God's. God is the larger context and plot in which our stories find themselves.[3]

As Jesus told the two travellers on the Emmaus Road The God Story he was giving them back their own. In realizing the Scriptures were one unified story leading to Jesus,[4] somehow their lives had never felt more meaningful.

We hope that through our attempt to tell The God Story you have been awakened to the reality that Sarah's barren womb, Jacob's wrestle with God, David's repentance after his affair, Daniel's prayers in Babylon, Mary's surrendered 'yes' to the miraculous conception and Peter's trance on a rooftop in Joppa have everything to do with your salvation. In the sovereign purposes of God, somehow the stories of these everyday-ordinary people who endured real-life circumstances like we do – joys and sorrows, births and deaths, successes and failures – breathe life into our everyday reality.

As we follow in their footsteps, offering our whole lives up to God, we come to realize somehow we are connected in a grand metanarrative that offers us a coherent worldview in a confused world. In the end we read the Bible so that the Bible will read us. Helping us find the story each one of us was born to live.

3 That you would tell and embody The God Story

As the eyes of the two friends on the Emmaus Road were opened and they recognized it was Jesus breaking bread in front of them, all they could do was go and tell the others what had happened.

Hearts burning and minds renewed, their feet ran with resurrection, telling their own story of encounter with the risen Jesus.

Our culture has exhausted itself. We find ourselves as a society morally bankrupt, unmoored from any anchoring story. The Christian story no longer forms the prevailing narrative shaping the attitudes and behaviours of our culture.

The world is telling our generation so many lesser stories. Each one of these 'stories' offers a different worldview. When we absorb these alternative scripts into our hearts and minds, even subconsciously, we become characters in a counterfeit story. Despite their best efforts these narratives are now proving to be built upon empty promises unable to deal with humanity's most fundamental problem: sin. The self-determining freedom that characterizes many of the world's big stories is not delivering the human flourishing it assured us it would. So much healing, forgiveness, reconciliation, peace and justice are still needed.

Dr Leonard Sweet is recognised for having said that the future belongs to the storytellers and connectors – and he is right. What if we never had a better chance to compassionately and confidently tell The God Story to a tired, anxious and disillusioned generation? What if, like those two on the Emmaus Road, teaching The God Story could lead our culture to a table, where bread will be broken and wine will be poured out? Through the words of the Scriptures the Spirit is wooing them there, ready to open their eyes to see Jesus and welcome them home.

The great missiologist Lesslie Newbigin once said that the business of the church is to tell and embody a story. After an encounter with Jesus, the Emmaus Road disciples moved from story-listeners to story-tellers. Jesus had told them The God Story. Now it was their turn. And now it is *our* turn.

We have an opportunity not just to be a part of history but also to shape history. Which means as you close the final page of this book you have an opportunity to step further into the story. The next words you speak, the next move you make, could help define the next chapters of God's eternal purposes still unfolding throughout history. Everything we do matters because everyone matters to the

Notes

Introduction

1 This is the word count for the NIV translation of the Bible. Obviously different translations have different amounts of words. Further, this is based on English translations and there are hundreds of Bible translations in other languages with different word counts.

1 The Origin

1 Gen. 1.1.

2 A. W. Tozer, *The Knowledge of the Holy* (New York: Harper & Row, 1961), p. 1.

3 Chris Green, *Surprised by God: Why and how what we think about the divine matters* (Eugene, OR: Cascade Books, 2018), p. 3.

4 Greg Boyd, 'A Brief Theology of God's Love', *ReKNEW*, 2016, <https://reknew.org/2016/08/brief-theology-gods-love/>

5 1 John 4.8.

6 Gen. 1.1.

7 Gen. 1.2–3.

8 Eugene Peterson, *Eat This Book: The art of spiritual reading* (London: Hodder & Stoughton, 2008), p. 93.

9 Gen. 1.3.

10 Ps. 33.6.

11 Heb. 1.3 NKJV (italics added).

12 In imperial measurements this equates to 186,000 miles (speed of light) and 25,000 miles (circumference of the Earth).

13 Ethan Siegel, 'There Are More Galaxies in the Universe than Even Carl Sagan Ever Imagined', *Big Think*, 2022, <https://bigthink.com/starts-with-a-bang/galaxies-in-universe/>

14 Ps. 147.4.

15 Gen. 2.2.

16 Gen. 2.3.

17 Eugene Peterson, *Christ Plays in Ten Thousand Places: A conversation in spiritual theology* (Grand Rapids, MI: Eerdmans, 2008).

18 Walter Brueggemann, *Sabbath as Resistance: Saying no to the*

culture of now (Louisville, KY: Westminster John Knox Press, 2014), p. 107.

19 Gen. 1.26–27 NRSV.

20 Gen. 2.7.

21 Gen. 2.7.

22 *Eikon* is the Greek word, derived from the original word for 'image'. This is instructive for us because *eikon* is where our English word 'icon' derives from. An 'icon' is a material object representing something or someone divine. Quite simply, humankind was created 'god-like'; 'little gods' actually isn't pushing it too far.

23 Ps. 8.4–6.

24 C. S. Lewis, *The Weight of Glory* (Grand Rapids, MI: HarperOne, 2001), p. 45.

25 Gen. 2.8.

26 Gen. 3.8.

27 Gen. 2.17.

28 Green, *Surprised by God*, p. 48.

29 Gen. 2.18.

30 Gen. 2.23.

31 Andy Crouch, *Strong and Weak: Embracing a life of love, risk and true flourishing* (Downers Grove, IL: Inter Varsity Press, 2016), p. 45.

32 Gen. 2.24.

33 Gen. 2.10–14.

34 Indebted to Greg Beale and Michael Hesier.

35 Gen. 1.28.

2 The Fall

1 Gen. 3.1.

2 Isa. 14.13.

3 Gen. 2.16–17.

4 Gen. 3.1–5.

5 Gen. 3.5.

6 Gen. 3.6.

7 Gen. 3.9.

8 Gen. 3.7.

9 Gen. 3.10.

10 Gen. 3.7.

11 Gen. 3.12.

12 Gen. 3.13.

13 John 8.44.

14 Ps. 51.5 KJV.

15 Augustine, *Confessions*, by Henry Chadwick (Oxford: Oxford University Press, 1991), p. 52.

16 J. K. A. Smith, *On the Road with Saint Augustine: A real world spirituality for restless hearts* (Grand Rapids, MI: Brazos Press, 2019), p. 214.

17 Gen. 1.28 ESV.

18 Gen. 3.21.

19 Gen. 3.15.

20 Gen. 3.24.

21 Gen. 4.16.

22 Gen. 4.14 MSG.

23 Gen. 4.15.

24 Gen. 4.15.

25 Gen. 4.24.
26 Gen. 6.5–6.
27 Gen. 6.9.
28 Gen. 9.1.
29 Gen. 11.4.
30 Gen. 11.7.

3 The Seed of Promise

1 Gen. 12.1.
2 Gen. 12.2–3.
3 Gen. 12.4.
4 Gen. 15.1.
5 Gen. 15.2.
6 Gen. 15.4.
7 Gen. 15.5.
8 Gen. 15.6.
9 Gen. 15.18.
10 Gen. 16.1–16.
11 Gen. 16.13.
12 Gen. 17.1–2 ESV.
13 Gen. 17.3.
14 Rom. 4.17–18 MSG.
15 Gen. 17.21.
16 Gen. 18.14.
17 Gen. 18.16–33.
18 Gen. 22.1–2.
19 Gen. 22.7.
20 Gen. 22.8.
21 Abraham's response unveils another name used to describe God in the biblical story. This is the first time *Jehovah Jireh* – God our Provider – is mentioned.
22 Walter Bruggemann, *Genesis: Interpretation: A commentary for teaching and preaching* (Louisville, KY: Westminster John Knox Press, 2010), pp. 134–45.
23 The Bible Project, <https://bibleproject.com/explore/video/abraham-and-melchizedek/>, has helped inform our thinking on this event.
24 Gen. 22.11–12.
25 Gen. 28.13.
26 Gen. 32.26.
27 Gen. 32.28.
28 Gen. 50.20 ESV.

4 The Birth of a Nation

1 Exod. 1.8 ESV.
2 Gen. 15.13–16.
3 'Hebrew' was a term used to describe an ancient semi-nomadic Semitic people basically synonymous with the children of Israel in the biblical narrative.
4 Exod. 3.3.
5 Exod. 3.4.
6 The six people we know of in the biblical story who respond with the phrase, 'Here I am,' are Abraham, Jacob, Moses, Samuel, Isaiah and Ananias.
7 Exod. 3.4.
8 Exod. 3.6.
9 Exod. 3.7–8.
10 Exod. 3.10.

11 Exod. 3.11.

12 Gen. 3.12.

13 Gen. 3.12.

14 Exod. 3.13.

15 Exod. 3.14.

16 C. S. Lewis, *The Problem of Pain* (New York: Touchstone, 1996), p. 37.

17 Exod. 3.15.

18 Exod. 14.13–14.

19 Exod. 15.2 ESV.

20 Gen. 15.18.

21 Exod. 16.3.

22 Exod. 19.3–6.

23 Rabbi Jonathan Sachs, *Covenant and Conversation; Leviticus: The book of holiness* (New Milford, CT: Toby Press, 2015), p. 5.

24 Philip Greenslade, *A Passion for God's Story: Your place in God's strategic plan* (Carlisle: Paternoster, 2002), p. 101.

25 Exod. 24.7.

26 Lev. 19.18.

27 Exod. 25.8.

28 Exod. 32.12.

29 Exod. 32.14.

30 Exod. 33.15.

31 Exod. 33.17.

32 Exod. 33.18.

33 Exod. 34.6–7.

34 Num. 14.7–8.

35 The chronology of the 40 years in the wilderness through the biblical texts is:

Exodus 19—Numbers 10: 1 year; Numbers 11—25: 38 years; Numbers 26—end of Deuteronomy: 1 year.

36 Deut. 34.6.

5 The Rise and Fall of the Kingdom of Israel

1 Josh. 1.2 ESV.

2 Exod. 33.11.

3 Josh. 1.5.

4 Josh. 1.6.

5 Josh. 3.16 ESV.

6 Josh. 5.9.

7 Josh. 5.12.

8 Josh. 5.13.

9 Josh. 5.14.

10 Josh. 5.15.

11 Josh. 24.15.

12 Josh. 24.23.

13 Josh. 24.31.

14 Josh. 21.43–45.

15 Judg. 2.10–12.

16 Judg. 2.19.

17 Judg. 15.15–17.

18 Judg. 17.6; 21.25.

19 1 Sam. 3.1.

20 1 Sam. 1.15.

21 1 Sam. 3.1, 3.

22 1 Sam. 3.10–11.

23 1 Sam. 8.7.

24 Thankful to Scot McKnight for this language of Plan A and Plan B in his book *Kingdom Conspiracy: Returning to the radical mission of the local*

church (Grand Rapids, MI:
Brazos Press, 2014).

25 1 Sam. 16.1.
26 1 Sam. 13.14.
27 1 Sam. 16.7.
28 1 Sam. 16.11.
29 1 Sam. 16.12.
30 Ps. 27.13.
31 Ps. 27.4 NKJV.
32 Ps. 63.1, 3.
33 2 Sam. 7.12, 16.
34 Ps. 51.10.
35 1 Kings 11.1 MSG.
36 1 Kings 15:26; 16:19, 30; 21:25;
   2 Kings 14:24.

6 The Prophets and Exile

1 Jer. 3.19–20 NLT.
2 Amos 3.7 ESV.
3 Abraham Joshua Heschel,
   The Prophets (New York, NY:
   HarperPerennial, 2001).
4 Indebted to Brian Zahnd for
   this definition.
5 Hos. 2.4–5 ESV.
6 Hos. 2.14–15 ESV.
7 Hos. 7.7; 8.14.
8 Jer. 3.6–11.
9 Jer. 29.14.
10 Dan. 1.8.
11 Dan. 2.44.
12 Jer. 29.11 ESV.
13 Jer. 29.7.
14 Ezek. 1.1.
15 Ezek. 47.
16 Ezek. 47.6 MSG.

17 Ezek. 47.1.
18 Ezek. 47.9.
19 Fleming Rutledge, The
   Crucifixion: Understanding the
   death of Jesus Christ (Grand
   Rapids, MI: Eerdmans, 2017),
   p. 140.
20 Isa. 57.15 MSG.
21 Isa. 49.6 NRSV.
22 Isa. 43.19 ESV.
23 Jer. 31.31 ESV.
24 Ezek. 36.26–27.
25 Isa. 42.1–4; 49.1–6; 50.4–11;
   52.13—53.12.
26 Hag. 1.4.
27 Ezra 10.1.
28 Mal. 4.5–6.

Interlude – the Silence

1 Eugene Peterson, Christ
   Plays in Ten Thousand Places:
   A conversation in spiritual
   theology (Grand Rapids, MI:
   Eerdmans, 2008).
2 'Ancient Near East' denotes
   a way of describing the great
   civilizations of the greater
   Mesopotamian region, of which
   Israel and Palestine were a part.
3 Grateful to Scot McKnight's
   teaching for helping shape
   these points.
4 Frederick Buechner, Listening
   to Your Life: Daily meditations
   with Frederick Buechner (New
   York: Harper One, 1992), p. 23.

7 The Son

1 Isa. 9.6.
2 Luke 1.17.
3 Luke 1.30–31, 34
4 Luke 1.35.
5 Luke 1.38.
6 Matt. 1.19 NRSV.
7 Matt. 1.20–23.
8 Pete Greig, *Dirty Glory: Go where your best prayers take you* (London: Hodder & Stoughton, 2018), p. 2.
9 John 1.14.
10 Luke 2.10–11.
11 Luke 2.14 NKJV.
12 Luke 2.30–32 MSG.
13 Luke 2.49 NKJV.
14 Luke 2.52.
15 Isa. 40.3.
16 Mal. 3.1; 4.5.
17 Matt. 3.5.
18 Matt. 3.7–8.
19 Matt. 3.11 MSG.
20 John 3.30.
21 The only place we see all three members of the Trinity active together.
22 Matt. 3.17 ESV.

8 The King

1 Mark 1.12–13.
2 Matt. 4.2.
3 Matt. 4.3.
4 Matt. 4.4.
5 Matt. 4.6.
6 Matt. 4.7.
7 Matt. 4.9.
8 Matt. 4.10.
9 Luke 4.14, 16.
10 Luke 4.18–19.
11 Luke 4.20.
12 Luke 4.21.
13 Luke 4.22.
14 1 Sam. 10:1, 6; 16:13, respectively.
15 Luke 8.1–3.
16 Matt. 4.17; Mark 1.15.
17 Luke 12.32 NLT.
18 Matt. 6.33 ESV.
19 John 7.46.
20 Robert Jenson, *A Theology in Outline: Can these bones live?* (New York: Oxford University Press, 2016), p. 27.
21 John 6.63.
22 Matt. 5.3–12.
23 Matt. 5.17.
24 Matt. 22.35–36.
25 Matt. 22.37–38.
26 Matt. 22.39.
27 Matt. 22.40.
28 People representing categories the Torah had declared unclean – lepers, the bleeding woman, dead people – Jesus touched.
29 John 14.9.
30 John 21.25.
31 Matt. 15.30.
32 Matt. 16.16.
33 2 Sam. 7; Pss. 2; 110.
34 Matt. 16.17.

35 Isa. 52.13—53.12.

36 Matt. 16.22–23.

9 The Passion

1 John Donne, *The Showing Forth of Christ: Sermons from John Donne.*

2 Zech. 9.9.

3 Matt. 21.13, quoting Isa. 56.7 and Jer. 7.11.

4 Matt. 21.33–46.

5 Mark 14.6.

6 Luke 22.15.

7 John's Gospel chapters 13–17 in particular record these discourses.

8 John 14.23.

9 John 15.15.

10 John 15.1, 5, 9.

11 *Paraclete* is the original Greek word meaning 'advocate' or 'helper'.

12 John 17.5, 24.

13 John 17.22–23.

14 Luke 22.19.

15 Luke 22.20.

16 Mark 14.34.

17 Mark 14.36.

18 John 19.5.

19 John 19.6.

20 John 19.14.

21 Luke 23.34.

22 Luke 23.42–43.

23 2 Cor. 5.21.

24 Matt 27.46, quoting Ps. 22.1.

25 Fleming Rutledge, *The Crucifixion: Understanding the death of Jesus Christ* (Grand Rapids, MI: Eerdmans, 2017), p. 100 – was a great help to me in these thoughts.

26 2 Cor. 5.18, 19.

27 Isa. 53.4 ESV.

28 John 19.28.

29 Luke 23.46.

30 John R. Cihak, 'Love Alone is Believable: Hans Urs von Balthasar's apologetics', *Ignatius Insight*, 2011, <https://fatherdavidbirdosb.blogspot.com/2011/02/love-alone-is-believable-hans-urs-von.html>

31 Matt. 28.5–7.

32 John 20.13.

33 John 20.15.

34 John 20.19.

35 Fredrich Beuchner, *The Final Beast* (New York: Atheneum, 1965), p. 175.

36 John 20.25.

37 John 20.27.

38 John 20.28.

39 Song of Sol. 8.6.

40 Matt. 28.18–20.

10 The Church

1 Acts 1.4, 8.

2 Acts 1.11.

3 Acts 2.2.

4 Acts 2.3.

5 Acts 2.4.

6 Acts 2.8.

7 Willie James Jennings,
*Acts: Belief: A theological
commentary on the Bible*
(Louisville, KY: Westminster
John Knox Press, 2017), p. 30.
8 Acts 2.14.
9 Acts 2.14, 16–18.
10 John 16.7 GNT.
11 Acts 2.24.
12 Acts 2.37.
13 Acts 2.38–39.
14 Apostles – from the Greek word
apostolos meaning 'sent one'.
15 Acts 3.6.
16 Jennings, *Acts*, p. 72.
17 We read about Philip's exploits
in Samaria in Acts 8.5–25.
18 Acts 8.26.
19 Jennings, *Acts*, p. 82.
20 Isa. 53.7.
21 Acts 9.3.
22 Acts 9.4.
23 Acts 9.5.
24 Jennings, *Acts*, p. 92.
25 Acts 9.6.
26 Acts 9.15.
27 Acts 10.5–6.
28 Acts 10.13.
29 Acts 10.14.
30 Acts 10.15.
31 Acts 10.20.
32 Acts 10.34–35.
33 Acts 10.47.
34 Acts 11.21.
35 Acts 13.2.
36 Acts 13.3.

37 Eph. 2.13; 3.8 ESV.
38 Acts 16.9.
39 Acts 17.6 ESV.
40 Acts 28.30.
41 Acts 28.31.

11 The Revelation

1 Rev. 1.17.
2 Rev. 1.17–19.
3 Matt. 28.20.
4 Rev. 1.9.
5 John 16.33.
6 Matt. 24.6–8.
7 Rom. 8.22.
8 Rom. 8.19.
9 Rom. 8.23.
10 Grateful for The Message
translation of Romans 8 here.
11 Rom. 8.26–27.
12 Jas. 1.2–4 MSG.
13 Rev. 4.1.
14 Rev. 4.8.
15 Rev. 5.2.
16 Rev. 5.5.
17 Rev. 5.12.
18 Rev. 11.15.
19 Rev 1.9.
20 Rev. 14.12 ESV; see also Rev.
13.10.
21 Alan Kreider, *The Patient
Ferment of the Early Church:
The improbable rise of
Christianity in the Roman
Empire* (Grand Rapids, MI:
Baker Academic, 2016), pp.
1–2.

22 Rom. 5.3–5 ESV.

23 Heb. 12.1–3.

24 Sources are Ken Curtis, 'Whatever Happened to the Twelve Apostles?', 2010, <https://www.christianity.com/church/church-history/timeline/1-300/whatever-happened-to-the-twelve-apostles-11629558.html>; David Pawson, *Unlocking the Bible: A unique overview of the whole Bible* (London: HarperCollins, 2007), p. 1059.

25 Rev. 6.10.

26 2 Tim. 4.1.

27 Matt. 24.14.

28 Matt. 24.12.

29 Rev. 3.5.

30 Phil. 2.15.

31 1 Cor. 15.53.

32 Rev. 1.8 NKJV.

33 Rev. 21.1–5.

34 St Julian of Norwich, *Showings* (New York: Paulist Press, c.1978).

35 Phil. 2.10–11.

36 1 Cor. 13.12.

37 Rev. 22.17.

38 Rev. 22.20–21.

12 Conclusion: Stepping into the Story

1 Augustine, *Confessions*, translated by Henry Chadwick (Oxford: Oxford University Press, 1991), p. 24.

2 Alasdair MacIntyre, *After Virtue: A study in moral theory*, 2nd edn (Notre Dame, IN: University of Notre Dame Press, 1984), p. 216.

3 Eugene Peterson, *The Invitation: A simple guide to the Bible* (Colorado Springs, CO: NavPress Publishing Group, 2008), p. 11.

4 This phrase is taken from The Bible Project.

Copyright Acknowledgements

The publisher and authors acknowledge with thanks permission to reproduce extracts from the following:

Unless otherwise indicated, all Scripture quotations are from The Holy Bible, New International Version (Anglicized edition). Copyright © 1979, 1984, 2011 by Biblica. Used by permission of Hodder & Stoughton Ltd, an Hachette UK company. All rights reserved. 'NIV' is a registered trademark of Biblica. UK trademark number 1448790.

Scripture quotations marked ESV are from the ESV Bible (The Holy Bible, English Standard Version), copyright © 2001 by Crossway, a publishing ministry of Good News Publishers. Used by permission. All rights reserved.

Scripture quotations marked GNT are from The Good News Bible, The Bible in Today's English Version. New Testament © 1966, 1971, 1976 by the American Bible Society.

Scripture quotations marked KJV are from the Authorized Version of the Bible (The King James Bible), the rights in which are vested in the Crown, and are reproduced by permission of the Crown's Patentee, Cambridge University Press.

Scripture quotations marked MSG are from THE MESSAGE. Copyright © by Eugene H. Peterson 1993, 1994, 1995, 1996, 2000, 2001, 2002. Used by permission of NavPress Publishing Group.

Printed in the USA
CPSIA information can be obtained
at www.ICGtesting.com
CBHW072025230524
8966CB00006B/18